# The SPLINTERS of our DISCONTENT

## How To Fix
## Social Media And Democracy
## Without Breaking Them

*Essays by Mike Godwin*

*Edited and with an introduction
by Charles Duan*

ZENGER

**Published by:**
Zenger Press
71 Hauxhurst Ave.
Weehawken, NJ 07086

**Typesetting and Cover Design:** Glenn Hauman

A CIP record for this book is acailable from the Library of Congress Catalog-
ing-in-Publication Data

**ISBN-13:** 978-1-939888-75-4

*This book owes most to Michel de Montaigne, who taught me something about how to write essays, including the importance of grounding my writing in our shared past.*

*It is dedicated to my beloved wife, Sienghom Ches, the angel of my present and my future.*

# Contents

# Acknowledgments

I didn't quite realize I'd written a book until my colleague at R Street Institute, Charles Duan, pointed out to me that I'd done so. His effort to organize and edit the material gave this book most of its current form. I'm not entirely sure I'd have organized this material the way he has done—or even that I agree with everything he's said in his gracious introduction—but I'm enough of a pluralist to recognize that somebody else may have better ideas to get my messages out than I have. At any rate, I leave it to readers to assess whether this material comes together as holistically as I'd hoped. And I have to thank Charles for helping this book achieve liftoff.

I should also thank Eli Lehrer, president of R Street Institute, for giving me enough breathing space to pull this book together. Maybe it will be successful enough to persuade him to let me do another project with him!

Thank you, Glenn Hauman, for seeing your way clear to publish this book, and especially for making it the inaugural book for Zenger Press. (If the name "Zenger" doesn't ring a bell for any of you readers, look it up on Wikipedia.)

Thank you to my brother Terry and to his wife, Tina, for being patient and supportive during a rough period of family transition. Thanks also to my daughter, Ariel, for similar patience and for reminding me that I occasionally craft a funny line.

If my Mom were alive today, I'd thank her too, for teaching me so much about strength in the face of pain and adversity, and for the value of sticking to one's guns. I started writing the material in this book shortly before we lost her, and I can't help hoping that Anne Caroline Sadler Godwin—as she believed she would be—is watching over me as I write these words.

Even as my life has been transmuted by the research and writing that fed this book, it also has been transmuted by the love of my wife, Sienghom Ches, to whom I dedicate this book. When we first met in Phnom Penh four years ago, neither of us imagined that we'd find ourselves living as husband and wife on (literally) the other side of the world. I promise now that this book is done that I'll get back to my Khmer lessons.

*—Mike Godwin*
*March 2019*

# Introduction

## by Charles Duan

Words of great thinkers have never stood alone, but are inevitably advanced through commentary. Plato's dialogues are styled as conversations with Socrates. Coke's famed treatise, *Institutes of the Laws of England*, [1] opens in its first volume as a commentary on the treatise of Sir Thomas de Littleton. No Torah stands without the Talmud recording the debates of rabbinic scholars, and no Talmud stands without the *perushim*, the traditional collection of commentaries.

No commentary is the equivalent of the original thinker or original work, but commentaries serve a different purpose. The commentator has several different jobs: to simplify, reorganize, or reframe ideas; to test ideas against hypotheticals and push those ideas to their limits; and to apply ideas to real-world situations for the betterment of humankind. Blackstone's *Commentaries*, [2] as summaries of the common law, were notable not simply because they reiterated the nominal reports of English court cases, but because they made the common law accessible to the people. Commentaries do not simply restate the works of others, but apply original thinking to their antecedents, often reaching new and different conclusions that advance a dialogue of thought.

---

1   Edward Coke, Institutes of the Lawes of England (1628), https://catalog.hathitrust.org/Record/100714247.

2   William Blackstone, Commentaries on the Laws of England (1765).

Mike Godwin takes on the key role of commentator in this book, beginning with a focus on the insightful theories of free expression that Jack Balkin has developed in his legal scholarship about Internet-based freedom of expression. Godwin then uses those theories as a jumping-off point for investigation of the questions raised by social media, big tech, and free expression in the Internet era. In doing so, he makes this trove of Balkin's thinking immediately accessible to policymakers, thinkers, and ordinary citizens concerned about the future of podcasts, blog posts, Twitter feeds, protest videos, and all other parts of that collective universe we call "free speech" or "free expression."

This volume collects a dozen and a half of Godwin's works on free expression and Balkin's theory. It is arranged in four parts.

**Part I** provides background on the key features of Balkin's speech theory. In an initial three-part series titled *Our Bipolar Free-Speech Disorder And How To Fix It*, Godwin explains Balkin's argument of how the Internet has changed the nature of speech regulation. Traditionally, the argument goes, regulation of expression was the domain of the state, giving rise to a two-party negotiation between citizens, who sought to make expression, and the government, who wished to impose controls on expression. It was under this paradigm that the First Amendment operated—as a rule defining the respective rights and obligations between speakers and the government.

Today, however, the forum for the vast majority of speech is not the public square or traditional publishing outlets, but rather online platforms. Those platforms do not naturally align with the traditional two-party model of speech regulation, in which citizens and the government dispute control over expression. Balkin thus devises a three-party model, placing platforms and other online services in a league of their own, giving rise to a "triangle" theory of expression. The crux of Balkin's theory—and the bulk of Godwin's commentary here—is that it is vital to inspect the incentives that characterize the relationships among these three parties. What leverage can the government exert against platforms to control citizens' expression, for example? How can platforms subvert—or enhance—the people's desire for free expression? And perhaps most importantly, what factors will draw platforms to align more closely with the government, or with the people? Godwin's articles explore these questions and provide some initial forays into how to apply Balkin's triangle theory to current social media platforms.

The next article, *It's Time to Reframe Our Relationship with Facebook*, touches on a related aspect of Balkin's work: the theory of "information fiduciaries." In the context of the debate over privacy, Balkin draws parallels between online platforms on the one hand, which store data such as photos and blog posts on behalf of users, and financial institutions or law firms that store valuable resources on behalf of their clients. Noting that the law imposes "fiduciary" obligations of care and loyalty on the latter group of institutions, Balkin proposes that an analogous scheme might apply to online services with respect to user data. Godwin discusses the implications of this theory, and proposes the additional possibility of platforms, as fiduciaries, acting as representatives of their users. This remarkable proposal addresses long-standing questions of how third parties may protect the interests of their users from government surveillance, and it merits serious consideration.

Having outlined and supplemented the features of Balkin's theory of free expression in the digital age, **Part II** applies that theory to the contemporary debate over social media. In *Has Facebook Merely Been Exploited by Our Enemies?*, Godwin reviews two recent books that discuss social media's impact on society with respect to disinformation and an educated electorate. In Godwin's view, these criticisms underplay an equally, if not more, important role of social media: connecting people of similar interests or similar needs to form politically powerful constituencies. This role depends much on treating social media as separate from the government; that is, treating social media as an independent corner of the Balkin speech triangle.

That theme arises again in *Here Comes the Attempt to Reframe Silicon Valley as Modern Robber Barons*. There, Godwin responds to another critique of technology platforms that, in his view, also underappreciates the virtuous bond between platforms and users.

As an avid user of Twitter, Godwin writes several times about the platform and its role in the debate over social media. In *Twitter Sucks Because We Suck*, he acknowledges the criticism of Twitter's failure to deal with hate speech and other objectionable content, but makes a salient point: It is very difficult to deal with these problems in ways that reduce criticism rather than intensify it. Content moderation is hard for many reasons, which Godwin explains in the article. Accordingly, in a world where "we're not going to see any top-down editorial policy," Godwin concludes that "the best fix is still to remind users they can make their own decisions about what to say and what to hear."

Part of that last article was inspired by Godwin's Twitter dialogue with television producer David Simon. That dialogue also led to a virtual fireside chat presented in the subsequent article *Tech People Are the Last People I Would Trust to Regulate Speech*, in which Simon and Godwin talk about Twitter and online speech.

Those discussions of individual social media commentators lead up to perhaps the most ambitious work in this volume: Godwin's three-part series, *Everything That's Wrong with Social Media and Big Internet Companies*. The first two parts (and a portion of the third part) consider many of the criticisms levied against Internet platforms and new technologies. A discussion of each criticism and response is unnecessary in this introduction, but some themes are worth observing. In rebutting criticisms of social media and its ill effects on society, Godwin relies heavily on drawing analogies to pre-Internet practices. Criticisms claiming that online advertising has an unhealthy influence on online users, for example, are met with references to the same criticisms made against television and print advertising.

Initially, analogizing to pre-Internet history may seem contradictory to Balkin's project insofar as the triangle theory of expression is supposed to represent a change in the ecosystem of expression. Yet there is an important and remarkable consistency. Speech platforms, as Godwin observes, obviously predate the Internet; prior to online communications, there were television, radio, print, town criers. But Balkin's triangle theory of expression was not necessary in that era because, at least for the most part, publishers and speakers were aligned against government intervention on speech. Yet today, the assumption for online platforms is that they ought to align exactly the opposite way, acting as regulators in concert with government or even at government's behest. By placing platforms separate from the side of the regulators, Balkin's theory resists this modern impulse to assume that platforms ought to be quasi-governments (indeed, quasi-governments freed of the restrictions of the First Amendment), while recognizing the economic reality that platforms will not align with users in quite the same way that older media tended to do. By drawing parallels between platforms and older media, Godwin thus seeks to strengthen the magnetic attraction between users and platforms, further resisting the temptation to collapse platforms with government.

**Part III** turns from problems to solutions. Here, Godwin considers how to apply Balkin's theory to advance the interests of free expression and democratic principles in an age of social media. Starting with the third part of the *Everything That's Wrong* series, Godwin contemplates the role of education on critical thinking as well as transparency in advertising. In addition, he considers matters of user privacy and taxonomizes the types of data that social media companies might collect. He also argues that additional research into the effects of advertising are necessary to having an informed debate on online advertising. Similar ideas are present in the subsequent piece, *Are Facebooks Ads Controlling Us? A New Version of an Old Question.*

The remaining three pieces in this part of the book are Godwin's contributions to an online colloquium entitled *Is Social Media Broken?* The primary thesis that Godwin advances here is that "we should focus more on democratic institutions than on the purported problem of 'fake news' " or castigating social media for today's problems. Noting that social media has been exceptionally important to organizing political movements such as opposition to the Colombian FARC guerrilla group, he questions the view that social media is "broken" or that social media's primary value is in trivialities of "pointless babble." In his view, social media platforms are still "a work in progress," and the most important social policy for improving them is to "give them—and us—the space in which to grow up."

Balkin's theory plays a central role in Godwin's emphasis within the colloquium on the importance of freedom of expression. As Godwin notes, Balkin criticizes the traditional view of freedom of expression as limited in purpose to promoting political deliberation; instead he views the right of free expression as central to self-actualization and individual liberty—whether that right is exercised for political debate or for putting more cat photos on Facebook. It is on this foundation that Godwin builds a powerful defense of social media as the necessary modern forum for "actual, meaningful, valuable, non-phatic communication—including both political (Meiklejohnian) and cultural (Emersonian or Balkinian)." Thus, contrary to those who would tear down social media to stop fake news in the name of democracy, Godwin calls for fostering social media as a key part of preserving democratic values and the human right of free expression.

In the final article of this part, *If Facebook Is Really at War, the Only Way to Win Is to Put Ethics First,* Godwin offers specific prescriptions to social media companies (one in particular) to advance the interests of democracy and human rights. He first calls on Facebook "to stop treating critics—even the meanest, most unfair and most intractable ones—as combatants." Because the company is part of an ecosystem of expression, Godwin finds that Facebook must form alliances, coalitions, and friendships with others in that ecosystem. He also returns to Balkin's concept of information fiduciaries, arguing that Facebook ought to make a "long-term unbreakable commitment" with its users regarding their data. Indeed, he observes that users would likely view Facebook more favorably were the company to take on this commitment. At the same time, Facebook would enjoy an enhanced ability to resist government demands for user data. In short, Godwin turns Balkin's theoretical ideas into practical directions that can alleviate the very real crisis of confidence in social media today.

**Part IV** turns to a broader question: Why is protecting online expression important in the first place? With a mind to history, Godwin answers that question with reference to one of the great Internet speech cases, *Reno v. ACLU*.[3] Discussing the history of that case, Godwin observes that the most compelling arguments for persuading the Supreme Court of the importance of overturning online-speech-restrictive laws were arguments about online communities—the notion that the Internet is not just an information resource but a place where people can connect, interact, form friendships, develop alliances, and work together for the betterment of society. Keeping the online sphere as open as *Reno* made it in 1997, Godwin concludes, is still important today.

Calling for openness of expression on the Internet is a hard thing to do these days. In *One Year After Charlottesville's "Unite The Right" Riots*, Godwin recognizes that the reach of online speech has caused tragedies, and that policing online expression through private actions like domain-name revocations seems like an easy solution to the worst cases. Yet he worries that this quick fix may lead to a slippery slope in which traditional rights of expression are subordinated to the whims of a technology company's CEO. Instead, while many see the online public square as the problem, Godwin sees the public square as part of the solution too. The ability of tens of thousands of well-minded people to oppose hate speech or malfeasance or harassment or intolerance— whether in physical congregation or in virtual joinder—is a powerful tool, enabled by a powerful Internet, that cannot be ignored.

---

3   Reno v. Am. Civil Liberties Union, 521 U.S. 844 (1997).

Solutions to contemporary problems cannot solely focus on the online sphere, as Godwin observes in his review of Yochai Benkler's book *Network Propaganda*. In *Splinters of Our Discontent*, Godwin explains how Benkler's research demonstrates that modern concerns about disinformation campaigns and partisan media divides are not simply a result of social media, but in fact are in no small part the consequence of traditional media institutions such as newspapers and television. Though Godwin's article does not say so explicitly, its insight is perhaps the most important demonstration of the relevance of Balkin's triangle theory today. The complex tripartite ecosystem of expression is not merely an Internet phenomenon but rather applicable to an evolving world of expression in all forms, including print and broadcast. As Godwin concludes, "problems in our political and media culture can't be delegated to Facebook or Twitter"; solutions to such problems as fake news must be trained on the "epistemic crises" of the body politic as a whole.

I am thus pleased to present Godwin's commentary on Balkin—a volume that connects academic insight with practical policy. The articles here are substantially as they originally ran, so they may contain references that were timely when originally published but are somewhat out-of-date now. In several instances I have changed references to point to print sources rather than online ones, and have occasionally altered the text in view of those changes.

Charles Duan
Director, Technology & Innovation Policy
R Street Institute
Washington, D.C.

# Balkin's Paradigm of Online Speech

# CHAPTER 1

# Our Bipolar Free-Speech Disorder and How to Fix It:

## *Part 1*

This article was originally published in *Techdirt* on November 28, 2018, at https://www.techdirt.com/articles/20181127/22041141115/our-bipolar-free-speech-disorder-how-to-fix-it-part-1.shtml.

When we argue how to respond to complaints about social media and internet companies, the resulting debate seems to break down into two sides. On one side, typically, are those who argue that it ought to be straightforward for companies to monitor (or censor) more problematic content. On the other are people who insist that the internet and its forums and platforms—including the large dominant ones like Facebook and Twitter—have become central channels of how to exercise freedom of expression in the 21st century, and we don't want to risk that freedom by forcing the companies to be monitors or censors, not least because they're guaranteed to make as many lousy decisions as good ones.

By reflex and inclination, I usually have fallen into the latter group. But after a couple of years of watching various slow-motion train wrecks centering on social media, I think it's time to break out of the bipolar disorder that afflicts our free-speech talk. Thanks primarily to a series of law-review articles by Yale law professor Jack Balkin, I now believe free-speech debates no longer can be simplified in terms of government-versus-people, companies versus people, or government versus companies. No "bipolar" view of free speech on the internet is going to give us the complete answers, and it's more likely than not to give us wrong answers, because today speech on the internet isn't really bipolar at all—it's an "ecosystem." [4]

Sometimes this is hard for civil libertarians, particularly Americans, to grasp. The First Amendment (like analogous free-speech guarantees in other democracies) tends to reduce every free-speech or free-press issue to people-versus-government. The people spoke, and the government sought to regulate that speech. By its terms, the First Amendment is directed solely at averting government impulses to censor against (a) publishers' right to publish controversial content and/or (b) individual speakers' right to speak controversial content. This is why First Amendment cases most commonly are named either with the government as a listed party (e.g., *Chaplinsky v. New Hampshire*) [5] or a representative of the government, acting in his or her government role as a government official, as a named party (e.g. Attorney General Janet Reno in *Reno v. ACLU*). [6]

But in some sense we've always known that this model is oversimplified. Even cases in which the complainant was nominally a private party still involved government action in the form of enactment of speech-restrictive laws that gave rise to the complaint. In *New York Times Inc. v. Sullivan*, [7] the plaintiff, Sullivan, was a public official, but his defamation case against the *New York Times* was grounded in his reputational interest as an ordinary citizen. In *Miami Herald Publishing Company v. Tornillo*, [8] plaintiff Tornillo was a citizen running for a state-government office who invoked a state-mandated "right of reply" because he had wanted to compel the Herald to print his responses to editorials that were critical of

---

4   Lee Rainie et al., "The Future of Free Speech, Trolls, Anonymity and Fake News On-line", Pew Res. Center: Internet Sci. & Tech (Mar. 29, 2017), http://www.pewinternet.org/2017/03/29/the-future-of-free-speech-trolls-anonymity-and-fake-news-online/.

5   Chaplinsky v. New Hampshire, 315 U.S. 568 (1942).

6   Reno, 521 U.S. 844.

7   N.Y. Times Co. v. Sullivan, 376 U.S. 254 (1964).

8   Miami Herald Publ'g Co. v. Tornillo, 418 U.S. 241 (1974).

his candidacy. In each of these cases, the plaintiff's demand did not itself represent a direct exercise of government power. The private plaintiffs' complaints were personal to them. Nevertheless, in each of these cases, the role of government (in protecting reputation as a valid legal interest, and in providing a political candidate a right of reply) was deemed by the Supreme Court to represent exercises of governmental power. For this reason, the Court concluded that these cases, despite their superficial focus on a private plaintiff's cause of action, nonetheless fall under the scope of the First Amendment. Both newspaper defendants won their Supreme Court appeals.

By contrast, private speech-related disputes between private entities, such as companies or individuals, normally are not judged as directly raising First Amendment issues. In the internet era, if a platform like Facebook or Twitter chooses to censor content or deny service to a subscriber because of (an asserted) violation of its Terms of Service, or if a platform like Google chooses to delist a website [9] that offers pharmaceutical drugs in violation of U.S. law or the law of other nations, any subsequent dispute is typically understood, at least initially, as a disagreement that does not raise First Amendment questions.

But the intersection between governmental action and private platforms and publishers has become both broader and blurrier in the course of the last decade. Partly this is because some platforms have become primary channels of communication for many individuals and businesses, and some of these platforms have become dominant in their markets. It is also due in part to concern about various ways the platforms have been employed with the goal of abusing individuals or groups, perpetrating fraud or other crimes, generating political unrest, or causing or increasing the probability of other socially harmful phenomena (including disinformation such as "fake news.")

To some extent, the increasing role of internet platforms, including but not limited to social media such as Facebook and Twitter in Western developed countries, as one of the primary media for free expression was predictable. (For example, in *Cyber Rights: Defending Free Speech in the Digital Age*, [10] I wrote this: "Increasingly, citizens of the world will be getting their news from computer-based communications-electronic

---

9   *Healthcare and medicines - Advertising Policies Help*, Google Support, https://support.google.com/adspolicy/answer/176031?hl=en.

10   Godwin, Mike. *Cyber Rights: Defending Free Speech in the Digital Age*. MIT Press, 2003.

bulletin boards, conferencing services, and networks-which differ institutionally from traditional print media and broadcast journalism." See also *Net Backlash = Fear of Freedom*: "For many journalists, 'freedom of the press' is a privilege that can't be entrusted to just anybody. And yet the Net does just that. At least potentially, pretty much anybody can say anything online—and it is almost impossible to shut them up." [11] )

What was perhaps less predictable, prior to the rise of market-dominant social-media platforms, is that government demands regarding content may result in "private governance" (where market-dominant companies become the agents of government demands but implement those demands less transparently than enacted legislation or recorded court cases do). What this has meant is that individual citizens concerned about exercising their freedom of expression in the internet era may find that exercising one's option to "exit" (in the Albert O. Hirschman sense [12]) may impose great costs.

At the same time, lack of transparency about platform policy (and private government) may make it difficult for individual speakers to interpret what laws or policies the censorship of their content (or the exclusion of themselves or others) in ways that enable them to give effective "voice" to their complaints. For example, they may infer that their censorship or "deplatforming" represents a political preference that has the effect of "silencing" their dissident views, which in a traditional public forum might be clearly understood as protected by First Amendment-grounded free-speech principles.

These perplexities, and the current public debates about freedom of speech on the internet, create the need for a reconsideration of the internet free speech not as a simplistic dyad, or as a set of simplistic, self-contained dyads, but instead as an ecosystem in which decisions in one part may well lead to unexpected, undesired effects in other parts. A better approach would be to consider internet freedom of expression "ecologically," to consider expression on the internet an "ecosystem," and to think about various legal, regulatory, policy, and economic choices as "free-speech environmentalists," with the underlying goal of protecting the internet free-speech ecosystem in ways that protect individuals' fundamental rights.

---

11  Mike Godwin, *Net Backlash=Fear of Freedom*, Wired (Aug. 2, 1995), https://www.wired.com/1995/08/net-backlashfear-freedom/.

12  Albert O. Hirschman, Exit, Voice, and Loyalty: Responses to Decline in Firms, Organizations, and States (1972).

Of course, individuals have more fundamental rights than freedom of expression. Notably, there is an international consensus that individuals deserve, inter alia, some kind of rights to privacy, although, as with expression, there is some disagreement about what the scope of privacy rights should be. But changing the consensus paradigm of freedom of expression so that it is understood as an ecosystem not only will improve law, regulation, and policy regarding free speech, but also will provide a model that possibly may be fruitful in other areas, like privacy.

In short, we need a theory of free speech that takes into account complexity. We need to build consensus around that theory so that stakeholders with a wide range of political beliefs nevertheless share a commitment to the complexity-accommodating paradigm. In order to do this, we need to begin with a taxonomy of stakeholders. Once we have the taxonomy, we need to identify how the players interact with one another. And ultimately we need some initiatives that suggest how we may address free-speech issues in ways that are not shortsighted, reactive, and reductive, but forward-looking, prospective, and inclusive.

*Figure 1.1: Balkin's pluralistic model of free speech.*

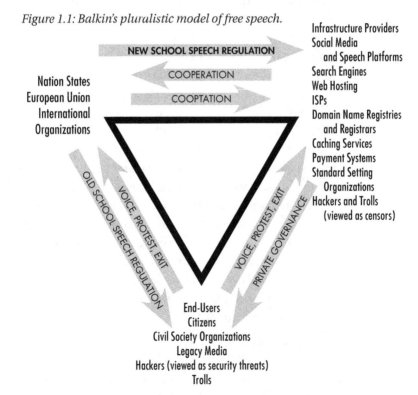

**The internet ecosystem: a taxonomy.**  Fortunately, Jack Balkin's recent series of law-review articles has given us a head start on building that theory, outlining the complex relationships that now exist among citizens, government actors, and companies that function as intermediaries. These paradigm-challenging articles culminate in a synthesis is reflected in his 2018 law-review article "Free Speech is a Triangle." [13]

Balkin rejects simple dyadic models of free speech. Because an infographic is sometimes worth 1000 words, it may be most convenient to reproduce Balkin's diagram of what he refers to as a "pluralistic" (rather than "dyadic") model of free speech. It is reproduced in Figure 1.1.

Balkin recognizes that the triangle may be taken as oversimplifying the character of particular entities within any set of parties at a "corner." For example, social-media platforms are not the same things as payment systems, which aren't the same things as search engines or standard-setting organizations. Nevertheless, entities in any given corner may have roughly the same interests and play roughly the same roles. End-users are not the same things as "Legacy Media" (e.g., the *Wall Street Journal* or the *Guardian*), yet both may be subject to "private governance" from internet platforms or subject to "old-school speech regulation" (laws and regulation) imposed by nation-states or treaties. ("New-school speech regulation" may arise when governments compel or pressure companies to exercise speech-suppressing "private governance.")

Certainly some entities within this triangularized model may be "flattened" in the diagram in ways that don't reveal the depth of their relationships to other parties. For example, a social-media company like Facebook may collect vastly more data (and use it in far more unregulated ways) than a payment system (and certainly far more than a standard-setting organization). Balkin addresses the problem of Big Data collection by social-media companies and others—including the issue of how Big Data may be used in ways that inhibit or distort free speech—by suggesting that such data-collecting companies be considered "information fiduciaries" with obligations that may parallel or be similar to those of more traditional fiduciaries such as doctors and lawyers. (He has developed this idea further in separate articles both sole-authored and co-authored with Jonathan Zittrain.) [14]

---

13  Jack M. Balkin, *Free Speech Is a Triangle*, 118 Colum. L. Rev. 2011 (2018), https://columbialawreview.org/content/free-speech-is-a-triangle/.

14  Jack M. Balkin & Jonathan Zittrain, *A Grand Bargain to Make Tech Companies Trustworthy*, The Atlantic (Oct. 3, 2016), https://www.theatlantic.com/technology/

Properly, the information-fiduciary paradigm maps more clearly to privacy interests rather than to free-expression interests, but collection, maintenance, and use of large amounts of user data may be used in free-speech contexts. The information-fiduciary concept may not seem to be directly relevant to content issues. But it's indirectly relevant if the information fiduciary (possibly but not always at the behest of government) uses user data to try to manipulate users through content, or to disclose user content choices to government (for example).

In addition, information fiduciaries functioning as social-media platforms have a different relationship with the users, who create the content that makes these platforms attractive. In the traditional world of newspapers and radio, publishers had a close voluntary relationship with the speakers and writers who created their content, which meant that traditional-media entities had strong incentives to protect their creators generally. To some large degree, publisher and creator interests were aligned, although there are predictable frictions, as when a newspaper's or broadcaster's advertisers threaten to remove financial support for controversial speakers and writers.

With online platforms, that alignment is much weaker, if it exists at all: Platforms lack incentives to fight for their users' content, and indeed may have incentives to censor it themselves for private profit (e.g., advertising dollars). In the same way that the traditional legal or financial or medical fiduciary relationship is necessary to correct possible misalignment of incentives, the "information fiduciary" relationship ought to be imposed on platforms to correct their misaligned incentives toward private censorship. In a strong sense, this concept of information fiduciary is a key to understanding how a new speech framework is arguably necessary, and how it might work.

I've written elsewhere about how Balkin's concept of social-media companies (and others) as information fiduciaries might actually position the companies to be stronger and better advocates[15] of free expression and privacy than they are now. But that's only one piece of the puzzle when it comes to thinking ecologically about today's internet free-speech issues. The other pieces require us to think about the other ways in

---

archive/2016/10/information-fiduciary/502346/.

15   Mike Godwin, *Tech Companies Like Facebook Should Have to Safeguard Your Data Like Lawyers and Doctors Do*, Slate (Nov. 16, 2018), https://slate.com/technology/2018/11/information-fiduciaries-facebook-google-jack-balkin-data-privacy.html.

which "bipolar thinking" about internet free speech not only causes us to misunderstand our problems but also tricks us into coming up bad solutions. And that's the subject I'll take up in Part 2.

# CHAPTER 2

# Our Bipolar Free-Speech Disorder and How to Fix It

## *Part 2*

This article was originally published in *Techdirt* on November 29, 2018, at https://www.techdirt.com/articles/20181128/22021641127/our-bipolar-free-speech-disorder-how-to-fix-it-part-2.shtml.

In Part 1 of this series, [16] I gave attention to law professor Jack Balkin's model of "free speech as a triangle," where each vertex of the triangle represents a group of stakeholders. The first vertex is government and intergovernmental actors. The second is internet platform and infrastructure providers, and the third is users themselves. This "triangle" model of speech actors is useful because it enables us to characterize the relationships among each set of actors, thereby illuminating how the nature of regulation of speech has changed and become more complicated than it used to be.

Take a look again at Figure 1.1 on page 23.

---

16 Mike Godwin, *Our Bipolar Free-Speech Disorder And How To Fix It (Part 1)*, Techdirt (Nov. 28, 2018), https://www.techdirt.com/articles/20181127/22041141115/our-bipolar-free-speech-disorder-how-to-fix-it-part-1.shtml.

Although it's clearer when we visualize all the players in the free-speech regulation landscape that a "free-speech triangle" at least captures more complexity than the usual speakers-against-the-government or speakers-against-the-companies or companies-against-the-government models, the fact is that our constitutional law and legal traditions predispose us to think of these questions in binary rather than, uh, "trinary" terms. We've been thinking this way for centuries, and it's a hard habit to shake. But shaking the binary habit is a necessity if we're going to get the free-speech ecosystem right in this century.

To do this we first have to look at how we typically reduce these "trinary" models to the binary models we're more used to dealing with. With three classes of actors, there are three possible "dyads" of relationships: user–platform, government–platform, and user–government.

**(a) Dyad 1: User complaints against platforms (censorship and data gathering)**  Users' complaints about platforms may ignore or obscure the effects of government demands on platforms and their content-moderation policies. Typically, public controversies around internet freedom of expression are framed by news coverage and analysis as well as by stakeholders themselves, as binary oppositions. If there is a conflict over content between (for example) Facebook and a user, especially if it occurs more than once, that user may conclude that that her content was removed for fundamentally political reasons. This perception may be exacerbated if the censorship occurred and was framed as a violation of the platform's terms of service. A user subject to such censorship may believe that her content is no more objectionable than that of users who weren't censored, or that her content is being censored while content that is just as heated, but representing a different political point of view, isn't being censored. Naturally enough, this outcome seems unfair, and a user may infer that the platform as a whole is politically biased against those of her political beliefs. It should be noted that complaints about politically motivated censorship apparently come from most and perhaps all sectors.

A second complaint from users may derive from data collection by a platform. This may not directly affect the direct content of a user's speech, but it may affect the kind of content she encounters, which, when driven by algorithms aimed increasing her engagement on the platform, may serve not only to urge her participation in more or more commercial transactions, but also to "radicalize" her, anger her, or otherwise disturb her. Even if an individual may judge herself more or less immune from algorithmically driven urges to view more and more radical and radicalizing content, she may be disturbed by the radicalizing effects that such content may be having on her culture generally.[17] And she may be disturbed at how an apparently more radicalized culture around her interacts with her in more disturbing ways.

Users may be concerned both about censorship of their own content (censorship that may seem unjustified) and platforms' use of data, which may seem to be designed to manipulate them or else manipulate other people. In response, users (and others) may demand that platforms track bad speakers or retain data about who bad speakers are (e.g., to prevent bad speakers from abandoning "burned" user accounts and returning with new accounts to create the same problems) as well as about what speakers say (so as to police bad speech more). But there are two likely outcomes of a short-term pursuit of pressuring platforms to censor more or differently, or to gather less data (about users themselves) or to gather more data (about how users' data are being used). One obvious, predictable outcome of these pressures is that, to the extent the companies respond to them, governments may leverage platforms' responses to user complaints in ways that make it easier for government to pressure platforms for more user content control (not always with the same concerns that individual users have) or to provide user data (because governments like to exercise the "third-party" doctrine to get access to data that users have "voluntarily" left behind on internet companies' and platform providers' services).

**(b) Dyad 2: Governments' demands on platforms (content and data)**
Government efforts to impose new moderation obligations on platforms, even in response to user complaints, may result in versions of the platforms that users value less, as well as more pressure on government to intervene further. In the United States, internet platform companies (like many other entities, including ordinary blog-hosting servers and arguably bloggers themselves) will find that their First Amendment rights are buttressed and extended by Section 230 of the Communications Decency Act,[18] which generally prohibits content-

---

17   Zeynep Tufekci, *YouTube, the Great Radicalizer*, N.Y. Times (Mar. 10, 2018), https://www.nytimes.com/2018/03/10/opinion/sunday/youtube-politics-radical.html.

18   47 U.S.C. § 230.

based liability for those who reproduce on the internet content that is originated by others. Although a full discussion of the breadth and the exceptions to Section 230—which was enacted as part of the omnibus federal Telecommunications Act reform in 1996[19]—is beyond the scope of this particular paper, it is important to underscore that Section 230 extends the scope of protection for "intermediaries" more broadly than First Amendment case law alone, if we are to judge by relevant digital-platform cases prior to 1996, might have done. But the embryonic case law in those early years of the digital revolution seemed to be moving in a direction that would have resulted in at least some First Amendment protections for platforms consistent with principles that protect traditional bookstores from legal liability for the content of particular books. One of the earliest cases prominent cases concerning online computer services, *Cubby v. CompuServe* (1991),[20] drew heavily on a 1959 Supreme Court case, *Smith v. California,*[21] that established that bookstores and newsstands were properly understood to deserve First Amendment protections based on their importance to the distribution of First Amendment-protected content.

Section 230's broad, bright-line protections (taken together with the copyright-specific protections for internet platforms created by the Digital Millennium Copyright Act in 1998) are widely interpreted by legal analysts and commentators as having created the legal framework that gave rise to internet-company success stories like Google, Facebook, and Twitter. These companies, as well as a raft of smaller, successful enterprises like Wikipedia and Reddit, originated in the United States and were protected in their infancy by Section 230. Even critics of the platforms—and there are many—typically attribute the success of these enterprises to the scope of Section 230. So it's no great surprise to discover that many and perhaps most critics of these companies (who may be government actors or private individuals) have become critics of Section 230 and want to repeal or amend it.

In particular, government entities in the United States, both at the federal level and at the state level, have sought to impose greater obligations on internet platforms not merely to remove content that is purportedly illegal, but also to prevent that content from being broadcast

---

19   Telecommunications Act of 1996, Pub. L. No. 104-104, 110 Stat. 56.

20   Cubby, Inc. v. CompuServe Inc., 776 F. Supp. 135 (S.D.N.Y. 1991).

21   Smith v. California, 361 U.S. 147 (1959).

by a platform in the first place. The notice-and-takedown model of the Digital Millennium Copyright Act of 1998, which lends itself to automated enforcement and remedies to a higher degree than non-copyright-related content complaints, is frequently suggested by government stakeholders as a model for how platforms ought to respond to complaints about other types of purportedly illegal content, including user-generated content. The fact that copyright enforcement, as distinct from enforcement other communications-related crimes or private causes of action, is comparatively much simpler than most other remedies in communications law, is a fact that is typically passed over by those who are unsympathetic to today's social-media landscape.

Although I'm focusing here primarily on U.S. government entities, this tendency is also evident among the governments of many other countries, including many countries that rank as "free" or "partly free" in Freedom House's annual world freedom report. [22] It may be reasonably asserted that the impulse of governments to offload the work of screening for illegal (or legal but disturbing) content is international. The European Union, for example, is actively exploring regulatory schemes that implicitly or explicitly impose content-policing norms on platform companies and that impose quick and large penalties if the platforms fail to comply. American platforms, which operate internationally, must abide by these systems at least with regard to their content delivery within EU jurisdictions as well as (some European regulators have argued) anywhere else in the world.

Added to governments' impulse to impose content restrictions and policing obligations on platforms is governments' hunger for the data that platforms collect. Not every aspect of the data that platforms like Google and Facebook and Twitter collect on users is publicly known, nor have the algorithms (decision-making processes and criteria implemented by computers) that the platforms use to decide what content may need monitoring, or what content users might prefer, being generally published. The reasons some aspects of the platforms' algorithmic decision-making may be generally reduced to two primary arguments. First, the platforms' particular choices about algorithmically selecting and serving content, based on user data, may reasonably classed as trade secrets, so that if they were made utterly public a competitor could free-ride on the platforms' (former) trade secrets to develop competing products. Second, if platform algorithms are made wholly public, it becomes easier for

---

22   Freedom House, Freedom in the World 2019 (2019), https://freedomhouse.org/report/freedom-world/freedom-world-2019.

anyone—ranging from commercial interests to mischievous hackers and state actors—to "game" content so that it is served to more users by the platform algorithms.

Governments' recognition that protections for platforms has made it easier for the platforms to survive and thrive may wish to modify the protections they have granted, or to impose further content-moderation obligations on platforms as a condition of statutory protections. But even AI-assisted moderation measures will necessarily be either post-hoc (which means that lots of objectionable content will be public before the platform curates it) or pre-hoc (which means that platforms will become gatekeepers of public participation, shoehorning users into a traditional publishing model or an online-forum model as constrained by top editors as the early version of the joint Sears-IBM service Prodigy[23] was).

**(c) Dyad 3: People (and traditional press) versus government**  New, frequently market-dominant internet platforms for speakers create new government temptations and capabilities to (i) surveil online speech, (ii) leverage platforms to suppress dissident or unpopular speech or deplatform speakers, and/or (iii) employ or compel platforms to manipulate public opinion (or to regulate or suppress manipulation). It's trivially demonstrable that some great percentage of complaints about censorship in open societies is grounded in individual speakers' or traditional publishers' complaints that government is acting to suppress certain kinds of speech. Frequently the speech in question is political speech but sometimes it is speech of other kinds (e.g., allegedly defamatory, threatening, fraudulent, or obscene) of speech. This dyad is, for the most part, the primary subject matter of traditional First Amendment law. It is also a primary focus of international free-expression law where freedom of expression is understood to be guaranteed by national or international human-rights instruments (notably Article 19 of the International Covenant on Civil and Political Rights).[24]

But this dyad has been distorted in the twenty-first century, in which, more often than not, troubling political speech or other kinds of troubling public speech are normally mediated by internet platforms. It is easier

---

23  *Prodigy (online service)*, Wikipedia (last edited Jan. 25, 2019), https://en.wikipedia.org/wiki/Prodigy (online service).

24  Office of the High Comm'r, *International Covenant on Civil and Political Rights*, United Nations Hum. Rts. (Dec. 16, 1966), https://www.ohchr.org:443/EN/ProfessionalInterest/Pages/CCPR.aspx.

on some platforms, but by no means all platforms, for speakers to be anonymous or pseudonymous. Anonymous or pseudonymous speech is not universally regarded by governments as a boon to public discourse, and frequently governments will want to track or even prosecute certain kinds of speakers. Tracking such speakers was difficult (although not necessarily impossible) in the pre-internet era of unsigned postcards and ubiquitous public telephones. But internet platforms have created new opportunities to discover, track, and suppress speech as a result of the platforms' collection of user data for their own purposes.

Every successful internet platform that allows users to express themselves has been a target of government demands for disclosure of information about users. In addition, internet platforms are increasingly the target of government efforts to mandate assistance (including the building of more surveillance-supportive technologies) in criminal-law or national-security investigations. In most ways this is analogous to the 1994 passage of CALEA[25] in the United States, which obligated telephone companies (that is, providers of voice telephony) to build technologies that facilitated wiretapping.

But a major difference is that the internet platforms more often than not capture far more information about users than telephone companies traditionally had done. (This generalization to some extent oversimplifies the difference, given that there is frequently convergence between the suites of services that internet platforms and telephone companies—or cable companies—now offer their users.)

Governmental monitoring may suppress dissenting (or otherwise troubling) speech, but governments (and other political actors, such as political parties) may also use internet platforms to create or potentiate certain kinds of political speech in opposition to the interests of users. Siva Vaidhyanathan documents particular uses of Facebook advertising in ways that aimed to achieve political results, including not just voting for an approved candidate but also dissuasion of some voters from voting at all, in the 2016 election.

As Vaidhyanathan writes: "Custom Audiences is a powerful tool that was not available to President Barack Obama and Governor Mitt Romney when they ran for president in 2012. It was developed in 2014 to help Facebook reach the takeoff point in profits and revenue." Plus

---

25   Communications Assistance for Law Enforcement Act, Pub. L. No. 103-414, 108 Stat. 4279 (1994) (codified at 47 U.S.C. §§ 1001–1010), https://www.gpo.gov/fdsys/granule/STATUTE-108/STATUTE-108-Pg4279/content-detail.html.

this: "Because Facebook develops advertising tools for firms that sell shoes and cosmetics and only later invites political campaigns to use them, 'they never worried about the worst-case abuse of this capability, unaccountable, unreviewable political ads,' said Professor David Carroll of the Parsons School of Design."

There are legitimate differences of opinion regarding the proper regime for regulation of political advertising, as well as regarding the extent to which regulation of political advertising can be implemented consistent with existing First Amendment precedent. It should be noted, however, that advertising of the sort that Vaidhyanathan discusses raises issues not only of campaign spending (although in 2016, at least, the spending on targeted Facebook political advertising of the "Custom Audiences" variety seems to have been comparatively small) as of transparency and accountability. Advertising that's micro-targeted and ephemeral is arguably not accountable to the degree that an open society should require. There will be temptations for government actors to use mechanisms like "Custom Audiences" to suppress opponents' speech—and there also will be temptations by government to limit or even abolish such micro-targeted instances of political speech.

What is most relevant here is that the government may address temptations either to employ features like "Custom Audiences" or to suppress the use of those features by other political actors in non-transparent or less formal ways, (e.g., through the "jawboning" that Jack Balkin describes in his "New School Speech Regulation" paper). [26] Platforms—especially market-dominant platforms that, as a function of their success and dominance, may be particularly targeted on speech issues—may feel pressured to remove dissident speech in response to government "jawboning" or other threats of regulation. And, given the limitations of both automated and human-based filtering, a platform that feels compelled to respond to such governmental pressure is almost certain to generate results that are inconsistent and that give rise to further dissatisfaction, complaints, and suspicions on the part of users—not just the users subject to censorship or deplatforming, [27] but also users who witness such actions and disapprove of them.

---

26    Jack M. Balkin, *Old School/New School Speech Regulation,* 127 Harv. L. Rev. 2296 (2014), https://digitalcommons.law.yale.edu/fss papers/4877/.

27    Jason Koebler, *Social Media Bans Actually Work,* Vice (Aug. 10, 2018), https://motherboard.vice.com/en us/article/bjbp9d/do-social-media-bans-work.

Considered both separately and together, it seems clear that each of the traditional "dyadic" models of how to regulate free speech tend to focus on two vertices of the free-speech triangle while overlooking a third vertex, whose stakeholders may intervene or distort or exploit or be exploited by outcomes of conflicts of the other two stakeholder groups. What this suggests is that no "dyadic" conception of the free-speech ecosystem is sufficiently complex and stable enough to protect freedom of expression or, for that matter, citizens' autonomy interests in privacy and self-determination. This leaves us with the question of whether it is possible to direct our law and policy in a direction that takes into account today's "triangular" free-speech ecosystem in ways that provide stable, durable, expansive protections of freedom of speech and other valid interests of all three stakeholder groups. That question is the subject of Part 3 of this series. [28]

---

28  Mike Godwin, *Our Bipolar Free-Speech Disorder And How To Fix It (Part 3)*, Techdirt (Nov. 30, 2018), https://www.techdirt.com/articles/20181130/09421141141/our-bipolar-free-speech-disorder-how-to-fix-it-part-3.shtml.

# CHAPTER 3

# Our Bipolar Free-Speech Disorder and How to Fix It

## *Part 3*

This article was originally published in *Techdirt* on November 30, 2018, at https://www.techdirt.com/articles/20181130/09421141141/our-bipolar-free-speech-disorder-how-to-fix-it-part-3.shtml.

Part 1 and Part 2 of this series have emphasized that treating today's free-speech ecosystem in "dyadic" ways—that is, treating each issue as fundamentally a tension between two parties or two sets of stakeholders—doesn't lead to stable or predictable outcomes that adequately protect free speech and related interests.

As policymakers consider laws that affect platforms or other online content, it is critical that they consider Balkin's framework and the implications of this "new-school speech regulation" that the framework identifies. Failure to apply it could lead—indeed, has led in the recent past—to laws or regulations that indirectly undermine basic free expression interests.

A critical perspective on how to think about free speech in the twenty-first century requires that we recognize the extent to which free speech is facilitated by the internet and its infrastructure. We also must recognize that free speech is in some new ways made vulnerable by the internet and its infrastructure. In particular, free speech is particularly enhanced by the lowering barriers to entry for speakers that the internet creates. At the same time, free speech is made vulnerable insofar as the internet and the infrastructure it provides for freedom of speech is subject to legal and regulatory action that may not be transparent to users. For example, a government may seek to block the administration of a dissident website's domain name, or may seek to block the use by dissident speakers of certain payment systems. [29]

There are of course non-governmental forces that may undermine or inhibit free speech—for example, the lowered barriers to entry make it easier for harassers or stalkers to discourage individuals from participation. This problem is in some sense an old problem in free-speech doctrine—the so-called "heckler's veto" [30]—is a subset of this problem. The problem of harassment may give rise to users' complaints directly to the platform provider, or to demands that government regulate the platforms (and other speakers) more.

Balkin explores the methods in which government can exercise both hard and soft power to censor or regulate speech at the infrastructure level. This can include direct changes of the law aimed at compelling internet platforms to censor or otherwise limit speech. This can include pressure that doesn't rise to the level of law or regulation, as when a lawmaker warns a platform that it must figure out how to regulate certain kinds of troubling expression because "[i]f you don't control your platform, we're going to have to do something about it." [31] It can include changes in law or regulation aimed at increasing incentives for platforms to self-police with a heavier hand. [32] Balkin characterizes the ways in which

---

29  Dan Gillmor, *WikiLeaks payments blockade sets dangerous precedent*, The Guardian (Oct. 27, 2011), https://www.theguardian.com/commentisfree/cifamerica/2011/oct/27/wikileaks-payments-blockade-dangerous-precedent.

30  Ruth McGaffey, *The Heckler's Veto*, 57 Marq. L. Scholarly Commons 39 (1973), https://scholarship.law.marquette.edu/mulr/vol57/iss1/3.

31  Benny Evangelista, *Facebook faces growing government scrutiny in privacy scandal*, S.F. Chron. (Mar. 26, 2018), https://www.sfchronicle.com/business/article/Facebook-faces-growing-government-scrutiny-in-12782652.php.

32  Eric Goldman, *'Worst of Both Worlds' FOSTA Signed Into Law, Completing Section 230's Evisceration*, Tech. & Marketing L. Blog (Apr. 11, 2018), https://blog.ericgoldman.org/archives/2018/04/worst-of-both-worlds-fosta-signed-into-law-completing-section-230s-evisceration.htm.

government can regulate speech of citizens and press indirectly, through pressure on or regulation of platforms and other intermediaries like payment systems, as "New School Speech Regulation." [33]

The important thing to remember is that government itself, although often asked to arbitrate issues that arise between internet platforms and users, is not always a disinterested party. For example, a government may have its own reasons for incentivizing platforms to collect more data (and to disclose the data it has collected), such as with National Security Letters. Because the government may regulate speech indirectly and non-transparently, there is a sense in which government cannot position itself on all issues as a neutral referee of competing interests between platforms and users. In a strong sense, the government itself may have its own interests that themselves may be in opposition to either user interests or platform interests or both.

**Toward a new Framework** It is important to recognize that entities at each corner of Balkin's "triangular" model may each have valid interests. For example, governmental entities may have valid interests in capturing data about users, or in suppressing or censoring certain (narrow) classes of speech, although only within a larger human-rights context in which speech is presumptively protected. End-users and traditional media companies share a presumptive right to free speech, but also other rights consistent with Article 19 of the ICCPR:

> Everyone has the right to freedom of opinion and expression; this right includes freedom to hold opinions without interference and to seek, receive and impart information and ideas through any media and regardless of frontiers.

The companies, including but not limited to internet infrastructure companies in the top right corner of the triangle, may not have the same kind of legal status that end users or traditional media have. By the same token they may not have the same kind of presumptively necessary role in democratic as governments have. But we may pragmatically recognize that they have a presumptive right to exist, pursue profit, and innovate, on the theory that their doing so ultimately redounds to the benefit of

---

33   Balkin, *supra* note 11.

end users and even traditional media, largely by expanding the scope of voice and access.

Properly, we should recognize all these players in the "triangular" paradigm as "stakeholders." With the exception of the manifestly illegal or malicious entities in the paradigm (e.g., "hackers" and "trolls"), entities at all three corners each have their respective interests that may be in some tension with actors at other corners of the triangle. Further, the bilateral processes between any two sets of entities may obscure or ignore the involvement of the third set in shaping goals and outcomes.

What this strongly suggests is the need for all (lawful, non-malicious) entities to work non-antagonistically towards shared goals in a way that heightens transparency and that improves holistic understanding of the complexity of internet free speech as an ecosystem.

Balkin suggests that his free-speech-triangle model is a model that highlights three problems: (1) "new school" speech regulation that uses the companies as indirect controllers and even censors of content, (2) "private governance" by companies that lacks transparency and accountability, and (3) the incentivized collection of big data that makes surveillance and manipulation of end users (and implicitly the traditional media) easier. He offers three suggested reforms: (a) "structural" regulation that promotes competition and prevents discrimination among "payment systems and basic internet services," (b) guarantees of "curatorial due process," and (c) recognition of "a new class of information fiduciaries."

Of the reforms, the first may be taken as a straightforward call for "network neutrality" regulation, a particular type of regulation of internet services that Balkin has expressly and publicly favored (e.g., his co-authored brief in the net neutrality litigation).[34] But it actually articulates a broader pro-competition principle that has implications for our current internet free-speech ecosystem.

Specifically, the imposition of content-moderation obligations by law and regulation actually inhibits competition and discriminates in favor of incumbent platform companies.[35] Which is to say, because

---

34  Brief of First Amendment Scholars as Amici Curiae in Support of Respondents, U.S. Telecom Ass'n v. Fed. Commc'ns Comm'n, 825 F.3d 674 (D.C. Cir. Sept. 21, 2015) (No. 15-063), https://ammori.org/2015/09/22/first-amendment-scholars-amicus-brief-in-the-net-neutrality-litigation/.

35  Mike Godwin, *Everything That's Wrong With Social Media Companies and Big Tech Platforms, Part 3*, Techdirt (July 16, 2018), https://www.techdirt.com/articles/20180715/22144840240/everything-thats-wrong-with-social-media-companies-big-tech-platforms-part-3.shtml.

content moderation requires a high degree both of capital investment (developing software and hardware infrastructure to respond to and anticipate problems) and of human intervention (because AI filters make stupid decisions, including false positives, that have free-speech impacts), highly capitalized internet incumbent "success stories" are ready to be responsive to law and regulation in ways that startups and market entrants generally are not. The second and third suggestions— that the platforms provide guarantees of "due process" in their systems of private governance, and that the companies that collect and hold Big Data meet fiduciary obligations—need less explanation. But I would add to the "information fiduciary" proposal that we would properly want such a fiduciary to be able to invoke some kind of privilege against routine disclosure of user information, just as traditional fiduciaries like doctors and lawyers are able to do.

Balkin's "triangle" paradigm, which gives us three sets of discrete stakeholders, three problems relating to the stakeholders' relationships with one another, and three reforms is a good first step to framing internet free-speech issues non-dyadically. But while the taxonomy is useful it shouldn't be limiting or necessarily reducible to three. There are arguably some additional reforms that ought to be considered, at a "meta" level (or, if you will, above and outside the corners of the free-speech triangle). With this in mind let us add the following "meta" recommendations to Balkin's three specific programmatic ones.

**Multistakeholderism**  The multipolar model that Balkin suggests, or any non-dyadic model, actually has been addressed in different ways by institutionalized precursors in the world of internet law and policy. That model is multistakeholderism. Those precursors, ranging from hands-on regulators and norm setters like ICANN to broader and more inclusive policy discussion forums like the Internet Governance Forum, are by no means perfect and so must be subjected to ongoing critical review and refinement. But they're better at providing a comprehensive, holistic perspective [36] than lawmaking and court cases. Governments should be able to participate, but should be recognizes as stakeholders and not just referees.

---

36   Danielle Tomson & David Morar, *A Better Way to Regulate Social Media*, Wall St. J. (Aug. 19, 2018), https://www.wsj.com/articles/a-better-way-to-regulate-social-media-1534707906.

**Commitment to democratic values, including free speech, on the internet** Everyone agrees that some kinds of freedom of expression are disturbing and disruptive on the internet—yet, naturally enough, not everybody agrees about what should be banned or controlled. We need to work actively to uncouple the commitment to free speech on the internet—which we should embrace as a function of both the First Amendment and international human-rights instruments—from debates about particular free-speech problems. The road to doing this lies in bipartisan (or multipartisan, or transpartisan) commitment to free-speech values. The road away from the commitment lies expressly in the presumption that "free speech" is a value that is more "right" than "left" (or vice versa). To save free speech for any of us, we must commit in the establishment of our internet policies to what Brandeis called "freedom for the thought that we hate."

**Commitment to "open society" models of internet norms and internet governance institutions** Recognition, following Karl Popper's *The Open Society and Its Enemies* (Chapter 7) [37] that our framework for internet law and regulation can't be "who has the right to govern" because all stakeholders have some claims of right regarding this. And it can't be "who is the best to govern" because that model leads to disputed notions of who's best. Instead, as Popper frames it,

> For even those who share this assumption of Plato's admit that political rulers are not always sufficiently "good" or "wise" (we need not worry about the precise meaning of these terms), and that it is not at all easy to get a government on whose goodness and wisdom one can implicitly rely. If that is granted, then we must ask whether political thought should not face from the beginning the possibility of bad government; whether we should not prepare for the worst leaders, and hope for the best. But this leads to a new approach to the problem of politics, for it forces us to replace the question: Who should rule? by the new question: How can we so organize political institutions that bad or incompetent rulers can be prevented from doing too much damage?

Popper's focus on institutions that prevent "too much damage" when "the worst leaders" in charge is the right one. Protecting freedom

---

37   Karl Popper, The Open Society and Its Enemies (1945).

of speech in today's internet ecosystem requires protecting against the excesses or imbalances that necessarily result from merely dyadic conceptions of where the problems are or where the responsibilities for correcting the problems lie. If, for example, government or the public want more content moderation by platforms, there need to be institutions that facilitate education and improved awareness about the tradeoffs. If, as a technical and human matter it's difficult (maybe impossible) to come up with a solution that (a) scales and (b) doesn't lead to a parade of objectionable instances of censorship/non-censorship/inequity/ bias, then we need create institutions in which that insight is fully shared among stakeholders. (Facebook has promised more than once to throw money at AI-based solutions, or partial solutions, to content problems, but the company is in the unhappy position of having a full wallet with nothing that's worth buying, at least for that purpose. See "Can Mark Zuckerberg Fix Facebook Before It Breaks Democracy?"[38]) The alternative will be increasing insistence that platforms engage in "private governance" that's both inconsistent and less accountable. In the absence of an "ecosystem" perspective, different stakeholders will insist on short-term solutions that ignore the potential for "vicious cycle" effects.

Older models for mass-medium free-speech regulation were entities like newspapers and publishers, with high degrees of editorial control, and common carriers like the telephone and telegraph, which mostly did not make content-filtering determinations. There is likely no version of these older models that would work for Twitter or Facebook (or similar platforms) while maintaining the great increase in freedom of expression that those platforms have enabled. Dyadic conceptions of responsibility may lead to "vicious cycles," as when Facebook is pressured to censor some content in response to demands for content moderation, and the company's response creates further unhappiness with the platform (because human beings who are the ultimate arbiters of individual content-moderation decisions are fallible, inconsistent, etc.). At that point, the criticism of the platform may frame itself as a demand for less "censorship" or for more "moderation" or for the end of all unfair censorship/moderation. There may also be the inference

---

38   Evan Osnos, *Can Mark Zuckerberg Fix Facebook Before It Breaks Democracy?*, N.Y.er (Sept. 10, 2018), https://www.newyorker.com/magazine/2018/09/17/can-mark-zuckerberg-fix-facebook-before-it-breaks-democracy.

that platforms have deliberately been socially irresponsible.[39] Although that inference may be correct in some specific cases, the general truth is that the platforms have more typically been wrestling with a range of different, competing responsibilities.

It is safe to assume that today's mass-media platforms, including but not limited to social media, as well as tomorrow's platforms will generate new models aimed at ensuring that the freedom of speech is protected. But the only way to increase the chances that the new models will be the best possible models is to create a framework of shared free-speech and open-society values, and to ensure that each set of stakeholders has its seats at the table when the model-building starts.

---

39   *Censorship On Social Media*, NPR.org (Aug. 11, 2018), https://www.npr.org/2018/08/11/637865162/censorship-on-social-media.

# CHAPTER 4

# It's Time to Reframe Our Relationship with Facebook

This article was originally published in *Slate* on November 16, 2018, at https://slate.com/technology/2018/11/information-fiduciaries-facebook-google-jack-balkin-data-privacy.html.

If Mark Zuckerberg and Sheryl Sandberg are hunkered down this week strategizing how to handle a devastating cascade of bad press, you can understand why. Wednesday's in-depth *New York Times* story[40] documents how Facebook has consistently taken a "delay, deny and deflect" approach to addressing its critics—rather than, you know, fixing Facebook's real problems. A raft of other negative stories have followed, most picking up on selected details from the *Times* story, of which the most absurd include the attempt to blame criticism of Facebook on George Soros[41] and Zuckerberg's reported insistence, after Apple CEO

---

40 Sheera Frenkel et al., *Delay, Deny and Deflect: How Facebooks Leaders Fought Through Crisis*, N.Y. Times (Nov. 14, 2018), https://www.nytimes.com/2018/11/14/technology/facebook-data-russia-election-racism.html.

41 Julia Carrie Wong, *Facebook reportedly discredited critics by linking them to George Soros*, The Guardian (Nov. 15, 2018), https://www.theguardian.com/technology/2018/nov/14/facebook-george-soros-pr-firm-discredit-critics-crisis.

Tim Cook criticized social media companies, that top execs abandon their iPhones. [42]

But instead of trying to spin the company's way out of this week's new PR problem, Zuck and Sandberg should pivot right now and focus on creating a new public policy and legal framework for the company that would comprehensively restore public trust. What does that new framework look like? A series of journal articles by Yale law professor Jack Balkin, culminating in a forthcoming article for the Buffalo Law Review called "The First Amendment in the Second Gilded Age," [43] suggests some important steps we can take to reframe our relationships with both companies and government when it comes to today's internet. The basic idea is to create a new legal category—he calls it "information fiduciaries"— that is a better fit for the roles Facebook and other companies play as facilitators of our free-speech rights and trustees of our personal data.

Balkin's approach has the advantage of being holistic rather than piecemeal. In that sense, it's better than current reactive steps Facebook has already been taking, such as crowdsourcing the identification of fake news, or deplatforming particularly noxious speakers like Alex Jones, [44] or renewing promises to monitor its business partners for how they handle user data. Properly implemented, these steps should strengthen our free speech on the platforms while also strengthening protections of our privacy and autonomy.

Balkin, who holds the Knight professorship of constitutional law and the First Amendment at Yale, is one of the legal academics who recognized early on how the internet was going to change public discourse in this century. So it's no surprise that he is the founder and director of the Yale Information Society Project, an interdisciplinary program at the law school that covers a full range of issues at the intersection of law, technology, and society. (Full disclosure: I was a fellow at Yale ISP from late 2005 until early 2007, years before Balkin developed the legal approach I'm discussing here.)

---

42  Rex Crum, *Mark Zuckerberg tells staff to dump iPhones in tiff with Apples Tim Cook*, Mercury News (Nov. 15, 2018), https://www.mercurynews.com/2018/11/15/mark-zuckerberg-tells-staff-to-dump-iphones-in-tiff-with-apples-tim-cook/.

43  Jack M. Balkin, *The First Amendment in the Second Gilded Age*, 2019 Buff. L. Rev. (forthcoming), https://papers.ssrn.com/sol3/papers.cfm?abstract'id=3253939.

44  Will Oremus, *Facebook and Apple Moved the Goal Posts to Ban Alex Jones*, Slate (Aug. 7, 2018), https://slate.com/technology/2018/08/facebook-and-apple-moved-the-goal-posts-to-ban-alex-jones-thats-encouraging.html.

In "The First Amendment in the Second Gilded Age," Balkin writes that the "grand bargain of twenty-first century media" mostly doesn't directly raise First Amendment issues because the First Amendment governs speech as directly regulated by federal and state governments. Under the terms of that "grand bargain," Balkin writes,

> Privately-owned infrastructure companies will provide you with many different valuable services. They will provide you with a search engine that is nothing short of miraculous—that allows you to find anything you want virtually instantaneously. They will provide you with social media that allow you to publish and express almost anything your heart could desire. Indeed, they will encourage to publish, and to communicate with others, repeatedly and incessantly. End users get all of these services, all of this stuff—and they get it all for free. And in return, media owners get to collect their data, analyze it, and use it to predict, control, and nudge what end-users do.

That last bit, of course, is the problem. On the one hand, the private companies obtain our data freely (that is, we consent to give it to them, even though we may not always, or often, think through the consequences of this choice). In return, we get cool free services that let us stay in touch with our high school friends and even conduct research or political organizing. On the other hand, the companies need to make money in order to offer us these free services, and the easiest way to do that is to sell advertising. Ideally, that advertising is for stuff we are likely to be interested in, which is the central reason for the companies to gather data about our interests from how we use these services.

The need for the companies to make money in order to offer us free services also creates a potential hazard: Algorithmically enhanced advertising is used, critics like Tristan Harris insist, [45] to deprive of us of agency. In effect, the critics say, online advertising, together with addictive aspects of social media, robs us of free will. (This is an argument about advertising that predates search engines and social media. As I've written

---

45    Tristan Harris, *How Online Advertising Is Tricking Your Thoughts, Attitudes, and Beliefs*, Big Think (Apr. 11, 2017), https://www.youtube.com/watch?v=SlGb8Yk0b4E.

in Lawfare, [46] its major wellspring is a 1950s book by Vance Packard, *The Hidden Persuaders*.) [47]

Unsurprisingly, one leading narrative in the debates about how social media platforms and other big internet and technology companies handle our personal information is that maybe they just shouldn't gather it at all. It's a narrative that touches not just social media platforms and search engines but also the makers of devices like smartphones that, because how we constantly carry them with us, become repositories of where we've been, whom we know, and who we are. That view has the advantage of simplicity—it's easy to understand and easy to state. And this narrative informs some suggestions for reform. For example, early Facebook investor Roger McNamee has argued that Facebook and other services should simply cease gathering user data and move to a strict subscription model. [48]

But if we ended the data gathering altogether (and maybe ended advertising altogether), [49] it would have consequences. If the *New York Times* or the *Washington Post* quit using online advertising—or cut advertising entirely—it would necessarily prevent any ads from manipulating us, but it would also increase their direct cost to readers, maybe by twice as much, or maybe much more. The same is true for social networking and search companies. As Balkin points out, "A subscription model has disadvantages for social media companies, because it might produce a far smaller user base, and therefore less interesting and intriguing content that would keep end users coming back for more."

Of course, we know already that data gathering definitely can be limited by law, as with the European Union's General Data Protection Regulation, [50] which went into effect in May 2018. But the GDPR's

---

46    *Are Facebooks Ads Controlling Us? A New Version of an Old Question*, Lawfare (May 16, 2018), https://www.lawfareblog.com/are-facebooks-ads-controlling-us-new-version-old-question.

47    Vance Packard, *The Hidden Persuaders* (1957).

48    Roger McNamee, *How to fix Facebook: Make users pay for it*, Wash. Post (Feb. 21, 2018), https://www.washingtonpost.com/opinions/how-to-fix-facebook-make-users-pay-for-it/2018/02/20/a22d04d6-165f-11e8-b681-2d4d462a1921˙story.html.

49    Ramsi Woodcock, *Advertising is obsolete—here's why it's time to end it*, The Conversation (Aug. 20, 2018), http://theconversation.com/advertising-is-obsolete-heres-why-its-time-to-end-it-101639.

50    Council Regulation (EU) 2016/679 of 27 April 2016 on General Data Protection Regulation, 2016 O.J. (L119) 1, https://eur-lex.europa.eu/legal-content/EN/TXT/PDF/?uri=CELEX:32016R0679.

prescriptions for handling personal data are built around the presumption that any gathering of personal data is bad for users and citizens. That's not the only model for protecting users, and it might not be the best one.

If we're going to let companies have this kind of intimate contact with our information, can't we also empower them to be advocates for our privacy?

Balkin's alternative, the "information fiduciaries" model, says the companies that gather our data in order to subsidize services for users could adopt—or Congress or the courts could impose on them—a legal and professional relationship with users as, in effect, trustees of our personal data. Just as doctors and lawyers gather information about us in order to serve us better, the companies might be constrained by the creation of similar professional relationships based on the services they offer and the individual users they are serving. As "fiduciaries," Balkin argues, the companies would have "three basic duties: a duty of care, a duty of confidentiality, and a duty of loyalty." These are the same duties that doctors and lawyers have with regard to their clients. Care and confidentiality mean the companies holding your data need to keep it secure and not use it negligently in ways that might hurt you, even accidentally. A duty of loyalty—again, the same duty that doctors and lawyers are bound by—means that the company you trust with your data can't use it in ways that benefit the company while hurting your interests, as when Facebook contracted to share user data with Cambridge Analytica. [51]

Here's what Balkin's model would mean for us as users. We might still agree, in return for access to useful free services like Facebook and Twitter, to abide by the companies' terms-of-service agreements—the agreements that allow the companies to use the personal data we give them in limited ways (for example, to serve us ads or other content we're interested in). But if the terms-of-service agreements are a contract between the users and the companies, that contract doesn't define the whole set of duties the companies owe to us. Apart from the agreements, the companies would be bound to be careful with our data, to keep it confidential, and to never use it (or allow it to be used) against us. (A company like Facebook, which has also gathered information about

---

51   April Glaser, *The Cambridge Analytica Scandal Is Over and Nothing Has Changed,* Slate (May 8, 2018), https://slate.com/technology/2018/05/the-cambridge-ana-lytica-scandal-is-over-and-nothing-has-changed.html.

individuals who don't use the service, might even be bound to use the data it's gathered according to these ethical and professional obligations.)

At least with regard to subscribers, these three duties—care, confidentiality, and loyalty—would take precedence over contracts or terms-of-service agreements. Per Balkin, "This fiduciary duty arises out of a contractual relationship—the terms of service or end-user license agreement—that digital companies require of their end-users. But duties of an information fiduciary are not limited to the specific terms of Facebook's privacy policy—a complicated contract that few people have actually read." Balkin points out that if Facebook's duties were only the specific obligations spelled out in the terms-of-service agreement, the company "could make those duties vanish simply by changing its privacy policy, to take effect the next time an end user logs in." A better approach, he says, is to recognize that "these fiduciary obligations exist on top of the contractual rights of the parties." In other words, the agreements wouldn't, and couldn't, allow you to waive your right to expect the services to honor these duties.

The concept of companies as "fiduciaries"—trustees of our personal information—underscores the limits on what the companies should be able to do. But it also could empower these successful, well-capitalized enterprises to be powerful, effective advocates of protecting our personal privacy.

Companies might not want to take this role on—but then again, they might. Think how much stronger Apple's arguments in the San Bernardino, California, shooter iPhone litigation might have been if Apple could have said meaningfully that it has standing as a trustee of its users' privacy interests to argue against any obligation to crack iPhone security. At the very least, this would enable Apple to counter any government argument that its opposition to cracking iPhone security is merely a "deliberate marketing decision to engineer its products so the government can't search them, even with a warrant." [52]

How do we get to Balkin's fiduciary framework? One way this could be done is by a federal statute with the right incentives built in (similar to the Communications Decency Act's Section 230, [53] which

---

52    Danny Yadron & Spencer Ackerman, *Apple accused of trying to make iPhones "warrant-proof" in FBI case*, The Guardian (Mar. 11, 2016), https://www.theguardian.com/technology/2016/mar/10/apple-fbi-encryption-case-san-bernardino-privacy.

53    47 U.S.C. § 230.

conditions immunity of internet services on whether they originated the content). Another way might be through professional associations working with state governments (analogous to state bar associations and medical associations). Or it could be a combination of both. However it's implemented, we can do so on the principle that if doctors and lawyers are legally and ethically required to do no harm to patients and clients, it isn't too much to ask that the companies—professional experts in how our digital data can be used—should be bound by analogous requirements. (New data-gathering companies, like new doctors and lawyers, might consider buying malpractice insurance.) Plus, this framework need not be limited to just internet companies—it could include Apple, cable companies, Netflix, cellphone providers, and so on.

This leads to one obvious legal benefit—it could diminish or eliminate the third-party doctrine that allows the government to easily seize or subpoena your data if it's held by a service provider. *Carpenter v. United States*, which was decided in the summer and imposed Fourth Amendment limitations on when the government can seize your cellphone location data,[54] called into question the whole idea of thinking that once some company is holding your information, you have no "reasonable expectation of privacy" and therefore no Fourth Amendment privacy rights. Justices both in the majority and in the dissents recognized that in the digital age, third-party doctrine is a fig leaf covering massive government prerogatives to capture our personal data—but they disagreed, of course, as to what to do about that.

Balkin's "information fiduciary" model could turn the third-party doctrine, already weakened by the *Carpenter* decision, into an irrelevant legal relic of a simpler analog era. With a statutory and/or professional framework of fiduciary obligations for tech companies, we could simply argue that, if the companies have a ton of data about us, we're protected not only by the Fourth Amendment but also by professional codes of ethical conduct that bind the tech companies that have fiduciary duties to us. (Our courts disfavor giving government access to lawyer-held client information or doctor-held medical information. They ought to disfavor Facebook's doing so as well.)

---

54    Mike Godwin, *After the Supreme Court's Carpenter Ruling, Where Is the "Reasonable Expectation of Privacy" Heading?*, Slate (June 27, 2018), https://slate.com/technology/2018/06/after-the-supreme-courts-carpenter-ruling-where-is-the-reasonable-expectation-of-privacy-heading.html.

Another possible benefit might be that Apple, Google, Facebook, Twitter, and others might have standing as fiduciaries or trustees to defend our fundamental rights of speech and privacy. After all, as we know from a 60-year-old Supreme Court case, *NAACP v. Alabama ex rel. Patterson,* [55] our ability to speak collectively may depend on our privacy and anonymity. In that case, the Alabama state government tried to compel the organization to disclose lists of its members (including addresses and phone numbers and so on). The NAACP resisted, and the Supreme Court concluded that (a) the NAACP has standing to assert fundamental speech and associational rights on behalf of its anonymous members, knowing that if compelled to disclose membership this would have real-world consequences for those members, and (b) these fundamental rights are deeply grounded in the First Amendment. The case is obviously relevant in this century because our ability to speak freely online and our privacy online are so intimately related. Properly understood, the NAACP was a "platform" for political speech and action in 1958, just as Facebook and Twitter are today. The companies might have standing, just as the NAACP does, to assert that the free-speech rights of their subscribers depend on their fiduciary obligation to keep user data confidential.

The fact is, whatever our reservations about big tech companies, or internet advertising, or privacy, we use the advertising-subsidized platforms to engage in more frequent, and more public, speech than preceding generations of Americans ever could hope to do. If we're going to let the companies have this kind of intimate contact with our information—which often serves us well, as when we're shown advertising that genuinely informs and helps us, or when our documents and contacts are synced among linked devices—can't we also empower them to be advocates for our privacy, just as the NAACP has been for more than half a century? If the tech companies have fiduciary relationships—not just contractual relationships—with their users, the companies arguably have stronger legal standing to resist government commands to disclose user data.

Taken together, this reframing allows us to think maybe it's OK after all for Facebook or Google to use our info to serve ads to us based on our likely interests, or to find new potential members of our social networks, but not to manipulate us, give our info over to untrusted and

---

55   NAACP v. Alabama *ex rel.* Patterson, 357 U.S. 449 (1958).

unsupervised third parties like Cambridge Analytica, [56] gather info on us even if we're not users of their services, or be reckless about serving fake news to us. And Balkin's "information fiduciaries" framework may also incentivize the companies to actively engage, as Apple and others sometimes have done, as advocates for our privacy and free speech—provided we give them legal standing to do so.

At the very least, Balkin's framework addresses our current concerns over Facebook's and other companies' gathering and use of our personal data. But I think Balkin offers more than that. His articles have charted a possible path back to the common ground we all shared in *Reno v. ACLU*, [57] back in 1997, a Supreme Court decision that tech companies and users came together to celebrate. The Reno case didn't ignore the likelihood that the internet and other digital technologies would be disruptive and disturbing as we lived through the technologies' growing pains. The court's optimistic recognition of First Amendment protections for expression on the internet signified hope that we all would survive the bumpy ride of the internet's adolescence on the way to a maturity based on mutual trust among stakeholders. And if some companies' shortsighted behavior regarding our personal data has eroded that trust, Balkin has shown us one path to enable them, and us, to restore it.

---

56  April Glaser, *No Matter What Facebook Says, You Can't Clean Up a Data Spill*, Slate (Apr. 4, 2018), https://slate.com/technology/2018/04/facebook-cant-clean-up-its-data-spill.html.

57  Reno v. Am. Civil Liberties Union, 521 U.S. 844 (1997).

## PART II

# Perceptions of Online Speech and Social Media

# CHAPTER 5

# Has Facebook Merely Been Exploited by Our Enemies? Or Is Facebook Itself the Real Enemy?

This article was originally published in *Techdirt* on June 5, 2018, at https://www.techdirt.com/articles/20180531/14372939953/ has-facebook-merely-been-exploited-our-enemies-is-facebook-itself-real-enemy.shtml.

Imagine that you're a new-media entrepreneur in Europe a few centuries back, and you come up with the idea of using moveable type in your printing press to make it easier and cheaper to produce more copies of books. If there are any would-be media critics in Europe taking note of your technological innovation, some will be optimists. The optimists will predict that cheap books will hasten the spread of knowledge and maybe even fuel a Renaissance of intellectual inquiry. They'll predict the rise of newspapers, perhaps, and anticipate increased solidarity of the citizenry thanks to shared information and shared culture.

Others will be pessimists—they'll foresee that the cheap spread of printed information will undermine institutions, will lead to doubts about the expertise of secular and religious leaders (who are, after all, better educated and better trained to handle the information that's now finding its way into ordinary people's hands). The pessimists will guess, quite reasonably, that cheap printing will lead to more publication of false information, heretical theories, and disruptive doctrines, which in turn may lead, ultimately, to destructive revolutions and religious schisms. The gloomiest pessimists will see, in cheap printing and later in the cheapness of paper itself—making it possible for all sorts of "fake news" to be spread—the sources of centuries of strife and division. And because the pain of the bad outcomes of cheap books is sharper and more attention-grabbing than contemplation of the long-term benefits of having most of the population know how to read, the gloomiest pessimists will seem to many to possess the more clear-eyed vision of the present and of the future. (Spoiler alert: both the optimists and the pessimists were right.)

Fast-forward to the 21st century, and this is just where we're finding ourselves when we look at public discussion and public policy centering on the internet, digital technologies, and social media. Two recent books written in the aftermath of recent revelations about mischievous and malicious exploitation of social-media platforms—especially Facebook and Twitter—exemplify this zeitgeist in different ways. And although both of these books are filled with valuable information and insights, they also yield (in different ways) to the temptation to see social media as the source of more harm than good. Which leaves me wanting very much both to praise what's great in these two books (which I read back-to-back) and to criticize them where I think they've gone too far over to the Dark Side.

The first book is Clint Watts's *Messing with the Enemy: Surviving in a Social Media World of Hackers, Terrorists, Russians, and Fake News*.[58] Watts is a West Point graduate and former FBI agent who's an expert on today's information warfare, including efforts by state actors (notably Russia) and non-state actors (notably Al Qaeda and ISIS) to exploit social media both to confound enemies and to recruit and inspire allies. I first heard of the book when I attended a conference at Stanford this spring where Watts—who has testified several times on these issues—was a presenter. His presentation was an eye-opening, erasing whatever lingering doubt I might have had about the scope and organization of those who want to use today's social media for malicious or destructive ends.

---

58   Clint Watts, Messing with the Enemy: Surviving in a Social Media World of Hackers, Terrorists, Russians, and Fake News (2018).

In *Messing with the Enemy,* Watts relates in a bracing yet matter-of-fact tone not only his substantive knowledge as a researcher and expert in social-media information warfare but also his first-person experiences in engaging with foreign terrorists active on social-media platforms and in being harassed by terrorists (mostly virtually) for challenging them in public exchanges. "The internet brought people together," Watts writes, "but today social media is tearing everyone apart." He notes the irony of social media's receiving premature and overgenerous credit for democratic movements against various dictatorships but later being exploited as platforms for anti-democratic and terrorist initiatives:

> Not long after many across the world applauded Facebook for toppling dictators during the Arab Spring revolutions of 2010 and 2011, it proved to be a propaganda platform and operational communications network for the largest terrorist mobilization in world history, bringing tens of thousands of foreign fighters under the Islamic State's banner in Syria and Iraq.

And it wasn't just non-state terrorists who learned quickly how to leverage social-media platforms; an increasingly activist and ambitious Russia, under the direction of Russian President Vladimir Putin, did so as well. Watts argues persuasively that Russia not only assisted and sponsored relatively inexpensive disinformation and propaganda campaigns using the social-media platforms to encourage divisiveness and lack of faith in government institutions (most successfully with the Brexit vote and the 2016 American elections) but also actively supported the hacking of the Democratic National Committee computer network which led to email dumps (using Wikileaks as a cutout). The security breaches, together with "computational propaganda"—social-media "bots" that mimicked real users in spreading disinformation and dissension—played an important role in the U.S. election, Watts writes, helping "the race remain close at times when Trump might have fallen completely out of the running." Even so, Watts doesn't believe Russian propaganda efforts alone would have tilted the outcome of the election—what it did instead was hobble support for Clinton so much that when, when FBI Director James Comey announced, one week before the election, that the Clinton email-server investigation had reopened, the Clinton campaign couldn't recover. "Without the Comey letter," he writes, "I believe Clinton would have won the election." Later in the book he connects the dots more explicitly: "Without the Russian influence effort, I believe Trump would not have been within striking distance of Clinton on Election Day. Russian influence, the Clinton email investigation, and luck brought Trump a victory—all of these forces combined."

Where Watts's book focuses on bad actors who exploit the openness of social-media platforms for various malicious ends, Siva Vaidhyanathan's *Antisocial Media: How Facebook Disconnects Us and Undermines Democracy*[59] argues that the platforms—and especially the Facebook platform—is inherently corrosive to democracy. (Full disclosure: I went to school with Vaidhyanathan, worked on our student newspaper with him, and I consider him a friend.) Acknowledging his intellectual debt to his mentor, the late social critic Neil Postman, Vaidhyanathan blames the negative impacts of various exploitations of Facebook and other platforms on the platforms themselves. Postman was a committed technopessimist, and Vaidhyanathan takes time to chart in *Antisocial Media* how Postman's general skepticism about new information technologies ultimately led his younger colleague to temper his originally optimistic view of the internet and digital technologies generally. If you read Vaidhyanathan's work over time, you find in his writing a progressively darker view of the internet and its ongoing evolution, taking a significantly more pessimistic turn around the time of his 2011 book, *The Googlization of Everything (and Why We Should Worry)*.[60] In his earlier book, Vaidhyanathan took pains to be as fair-minded as he could in raising questions about Google and whether it can or should be trusted to play such an outsized role in our culture as the mediator of so much of our informational resources. He was skeptical (not unreasonably) about whether Google's confidence in both its own good intentions and its own expertise is sufficient reason to trust the company—not least because a powerful company can stay around as a gatekeeper for the internet long past the time its well-intentioned founders depart or retire.

With *Antisocial Media*, Vaidhyanathan cuts Mark Zuckerberg (and his COO, Sheryl Sandberg) rather less of a break. Facebook's leadership, as I read Vaidhyanathan's take, is both more arrogant than Google's and more heedless of the consequences of its commitment to connect everyone in the world through the platform. Synthesizing a full range

---

59   Siva Vaidhyanathan, Antisocial Media: How Facebook Disconnects Us and Undermines Democracy (2018).

60   Siva Vaidhyanathan, The Googlization of Everything (and Why We Should Worry) (2012).

of recent critiques of Facebook's design as a platform, he relentlessly characterizes Facebook as driving us to shallow, reactive reactions to one another rather than promoting reflective discourse that might improve or promote our shared values. Facebook, in his view, distracts us instead of inspiring us to think. It's addictive for us in something like the same way gambling or potato chips can be addictive for us. Facebook privileges the visual (photographs, images, GIFs, and the like), he insists, over the verbal and discursive.

And of course even the verbal content is either filter-bubbly—as when we convene in private Facebook groups to share, say, our unhappiness about current politics—or divisive (so that we share and intensify our outrage about other people's bad behavior, maybe including screenshots of something awful someone has said elsewhere on Facebook or on Twitter). Vaidhyanathan suggests that at one point our political discourse as ordinary citizens was more rational and reflective, but now is more emotion- and rage-driven and divisive. Me, I think the emotionalism and rage was always there.

Even when Vaidhyanathan allows that there may be something positive about one's interactions on Facebook, he can't quite help himself from being reductive and dismissive about it:

> Nor is Facebook bad for everyone all the time. In fact, it's benefited millions individually. Facebook has also allowed people to find support and community despite being shunned by friends and family or being geographically isolated. Facebook is still our chief source of cute baby and puppy photos. Babies and puppies are among the things that make life worth living. We could all use more images of cuteness and sweetness to get us through our days. On Facebook babies and puppies run in the same column as serious personal appeals for financial help with medical care, advertisements for and against political candidates, bogus claims against science, and appeals to racism and violence.

In other words, Facebook may occasionally make us feel good for the right reasons (babies and puppies) but that's about the best most people can hope for from the platform. Vaidhyanathan has a particular antipathy towards Candy Crush, which you can connect to your Facebook account—a video game that certainly seems vacuous, but also seems innocuous to me. (I've never played it myself.)

Given his antipathy towards Facebook, you might think that Vaidhyanathan's book is just another reworking of the moral-panic tomes that we've seen a lot of in the last year or two, which decry the internet and social media much the same way previous generations of would-be social critics complained about television, or the movies, or rock music, or comic books. (Hi, Jonathan Taplin! Hi, Franklin Foer!) But that's a mistake, primarily because Vaidhyanathan digs deep into choices—some technical and some policy-driven—that Facebook has made that facilitated bad actors' using the platform maliciously and destructively. Plus, Vaidhyanathan, to his credit, gives attention to how oppressive governments have learned to use the platform to stifle dissent and mute political opposition. (Watts notes this as well.) I was particularly pleased to see his calling out how Facebook is used in India, in the Philippines, and in Cambodia—all countries where I've been privileged to work directly with pro-democracy NGOs.

What I find particularly valuable is Vaidhyanathan's exploration of Facebook's advertising policies and their effect on political ads—I learned plenty from *Antisocial Media* about the company's "Custom Audiences from Customer Lists," including this disturbing bit:

> Facebook's Custom Audiences from Customer Lists also gives campaigns an additional power. By entering email addresses of those unlikely to support a candidate or those likely to support an opponent, a campaign can narrowly target groups as small as twenty people and dissuade them from voting at all. "We have three major voter suppression operations under way," a campaign official told Bloomberg News just weeks before the election. The campaign was working to convince white leftists and liberals who had supported socialist Bernie Sanders in his primary bid against Clinton, young women, and African American voters not to go to the polls on election day. The campaign carefully targeted messages on Facebook to each of these groups. Clinton's former support for international trade agreements would raise doubts among leftists. Her husband's documented affairs with other women might soften support for Clinton among young women…

What one saw in Facebook's deployment of the Custom Audiences feature is something fundamentally new and disturbing:

Custom Audiences is a powerful tool that was not available to President Barack Obama and Governor Mitt Romney when they ran for president in 2012. It was developed in 2014 to help Facebook reach the takeoff point in profits and revenue. Because Facebook develops advertising tools for firms that sell shoes and cosmetics and only later invites political campaigns to use them, "they never worried about the worst-case abuse of this capability, unaccountable, unreviewable political ads," said Professor David Carroll of the Parsons School of Design. Such ads are created on a massive scale, targeted at groups as small as twenty, and disappear, so they are never examined or debated.

Vaidhyanathan quite properly criticizes Mark Zuckerberg's late-to-the-party recognition that perhaps Facebook may much more of a home to divisiveness and political mischief (and general unhappiness) than he previously had been willing to admit. And he's right to say that some of Zuckerberg's framing of new design directions for Facebook may be as likely to cause harm (e.g., more self-isolation in filter bubbles) than good. "The existence of hundreds of Facebook groups devoted to convincing others that the earth is flat should have raised some doubt among Facebook's leaders that empowering groups might not enhance the information ecosystem of Facebook," he writes. "Groups are as likely to divide us and make us dumber as any other aspect of Facebook."

But here I have to take issue with my friend Siva, because he overlooks or dismisses the possibility that Facebook's increasing support for "groups" of like-minded users may ultimately add up to a net social positive. For example, the #metoo groups seem to have enabled more women (and men) to come forward and talk frankly about their experiences with sexual assault and to begin to hold perpetrators of sexual assault and sexual harassment accountable. The fact that some folks also use Facebook groups for more frivolous or wrongheaded reasons (like promoting flat-earthism) strikes me as comparatively inconsequential.

Vaidhyanathan's also too quick, it seems to me, to dismiss the potential for Facebook and other platforms to facilitate political and social reform in transitional democracies and developing countries. Yes, bad governments can use social media to promote support for their regimes, and I don't think it's particularly remarkable that oppressive governments (or non-state actors like ISIS) learn to use new communications media maliciously. Governments may frequently be slow, but they're not invariably stupid—

so it's no big surprise, for example that Cambodian prime minister Hun Sen has figured out how to use his Facebook page to drum up support for his one-party rule, which has driven out opposition press and the opposition Cambodia National Rescue Party.

But Vaidhyanathan overlooks how some activists are using Facebook's private groups to organize reform or opposition activities. In researching this review, I reached out to friends and colleagues in Cambodia, the Philippines and elsewhere to confirm whether the platform is useful to them—certainly they're cautious about what they say in public on Facebook, but they definitely use private groups for some organizational purposes. What makes the platform useful to activists is that it's accessible, easy to use, and amenable to posting multimedia sources (like pictures and videos of police and soldiers acting brutally towards protestors). And it's not just images—when I worked with activists in Cambodia on developing a citizen-rights framework as a response to their government's abrupt initiation of "cybercrime" legislation (really an effort to suppress dissenting speech), I suggested they work collaboratively in the MediaWiki software that Wikipedia's editors use. But the Cambodian activists quickly discovered that Facebook was an easier platform for technically less proficient users to learn quickly and use to review draft texts together. I was surprised at this, but also encouraged. Even though I had my own doubts whether Facebook was the right tool for the job, I figured they didn't need yet another American trying to tell them how to manage their own collaborations.

Like Watts's book, Vaidhyanathan's is strongest where it's built on independent research that doesn't merely echo what other critics have said. And both books are weakest when they uncritically import notions like Eli Pariser's "filter bubble" hypothesis or the social-media-makes-us-depressed hypothesis. (Both these notions are echoes of previous moral panics about previous new media, including broadcasting in the 20th century and cheap paper in the 19th. [61] And both have been challenged by researchers.) Vaidhyanathan's so certain of the meme that Facebook's Free Basics program is an assault on network neutrality that he mostly doesn't investigate the program itself in any detail. The result is that his book (to this reader, anyway) seems to conflate Free Basics (a collection of low-bandwidth resources that Facebook provided a zero-

---

61   Rachel Adler, *The 19th Century Moral Panic Over...Paper Technology*, Slate (Aug. 4, 2017), https://slate.com/technology/2017/08/the-19th-century-moral-panic-over-paper-technology.html.

rated platform for) with Facebook Zero (a zero-rated low-bandwidth version of Facebook by itself). In contrast, the Wikipedia articles on Free Basics and Facebook Zero lead off with warnings not to confuse the two.

In addition to the strengths and weaknesses the two books share, they also have a certain rhetorical approach in common—largely, in my view, because both authors want to push for reform, and because they want to challenge with the sunny-yet-unwarranted optimism with which Zuckerberg and Sandberg and other boosters have characterized social media. In effect, both authors seem to take the approach that, as we learn to be much more critical of social-media platforms, we don't need to worry about throwing out the baby with the bathwater—because, really, there is no baby. (If we bail on Facebook altogether, it's only the frequent baby pictures that we'd lose.)

Even so, both books also share an unwillingness to call for simple opposition to Facebook and other social-media platforms merely because they're misused. Watts argues persuasively instead for more coherent and effective positive messaging about American politics and culture—of the sort that used to be the province of the United States Information Agency. (I think he'd be happy if the USIA were revived; I would be too.) He also calls for an "equivalent of Consumer Reports" to "be created for social media feeds," which also strikes me as a fine idea.

Vaidhyanathan's reform agenda is less optimistic. For one thing, he's dismissive of "media literacy" as a solution because he doubts "we could even agree on what that term means and that there would be some way to train nearly two billion people to distinguish good from bad content." He has some near-term suggestions—for example, he'd like to see an antitrust-type initiative to break up Facebook, although it's unclear to me whether multiple competing Facebooks or a disassembled Facebook would be less hospitable to the kind of shallowness and abuses he sees in the platform's current incarnation. But mostly he calls for a kind of cultural shift driven by social critics and researchers like himself:

> This will be a long process. Those concerned about the degradation of public discourse and the erosion of trust in experts and institutions will have to mount a campaign to challenge the dominant techno-fundamentalist myth. The long, slow process of changing minds, cultures, and ideologies never yields results in the short term. It sometimes yields results over decades or centuries.

I agree that it frequently takes decades or even longer to truly assess how new media affect our culture for good or for ill. But as long as we're contemplating all those years of effort, I see no reason not to put media literacy on the agenda as well. I think there's plenty of evidence that people can learn to read what they see on the internet critically and do better than simply cherry-pick sources that agree with them—a vice that, it must be said, predates social media and the internet itself. The result of increasing skepticism about media platforms and the information we find in them may also lead (as Watts warns us) to more distrust of "experts" and "expertise," with the result that true expertise is more likely to be unfairly and unwisely devalued. But my own view is that skepticism and critical thinking—even about experts with expertise—is generally positive. For example, it may be annoying to today's physicians that patients increasingly resort to the internet about their real or imagined health problems—but engaged patients, even if they have to be walked back from foolish ideas again and again, are probably better off than the more passive health-care consumers of previous generations.

I think Vaidhyanathan is right, ultimately, to urge that we continue to think about social media critically and skeptically, over decades—and, you know, forever. But I think Watts offers the best near-term tactical solution:

> On social media, the most effective way to challenge a troll comes from a method that's taught in intelligence analysis. To sharpen an analyst's skills and judgment, a supervisor or instructor will ask the subordinate two questions when he or she provides an assessment: "What do those who disagree with your assessment think, and why?" The analyst must articulate a competing viewpoint. The second question is even more important: "Under what conditions, specifically, would your assessment be wrong?" . . . When I get a troll on Facebook, I'll inquire, "Under what circumstance would you admit you were wrong?" or "What evidence would convince you otherwise?" If they don't answer or can't articulate their answer, then I disregard them on that topic indefinitely.

Watts's heuristic strikes me as the perfect first entry in the syllabus for media literacy in particular and for criticism of social media in general.

In sum, I think both *Messing with the Enemy* and *Antisocial Media* deserve to be on every internet-focused policymaker's must-read list this season. I also think it's best that readers honor these books by reading them with the same clear-eyed skepticism that their authors preach.

## CHAPTER 6

# Here Comes the Attempt to Reframe Silicon Valley as Modern Robber Barons

This article was originally published in *Techdirt* on April 26, 2017, at https://www.techdirt.com/articles/20170425/11120637235/ here-comes-attempt-to-reframe-silicon-valley-as-modern-robber-barons.shtml.

It's difficult for me to read Jonathan Taplin's *cri de coeur* about Google and other technology companies [62] that have come to dominate the top tier of successful American corporations without wincing in sympathy on his behalf.

But the pain I feel is not grounded in Taplin's certainty that something amoral, libertarian and unregulated is undermining democracy. Instead, it's in Taplin's profound misunderstanding of both the innovations and social changes that have made these companies not merely successful but also—for most Americans—vastly useful in enabling people to stay connected, express themselves and find the goods and services (and, even more importantly, communities) they need.

---

62   Jonathan Taplin, *Is It Time to Break Up Google?*, N.Y. Times (Apr. 22, 2017), https://www.nytimes.com/2017/04/22/opinion/sunday/is-it-time-to-break-up-google.html.

"It is impossible to deny that Facebook, Google and Amazon have stymied innovation on a broad scale," Taplin argues in his screed. He wants Google to divest itself of DoubleClick, in theory because the search engine would be much better if it were unable to generate profits from digitized ad services. He wants Facebook to unload WhatsApp, because the world was much better when connected citizens in the developing world had to pay 10 cents for each SMS message they sent. None of this really amounts to reform and, of course, such "reforms" wouldn't touch companies like Apple or Microsoft in the least.

What Taplin really wants isn't to reform but to reframe. He wants us to understand current tech-company leaders as evil, or at least amoral and out of control. Toward this end, he begins his new book (a much more extended version of his *Times* screed) by ominously quoting Facebook's Mark Zuckerberg: "Move fast and break things. Unless you are breaking stuff, you aren't moving fast enough."

Despite his misreading of the underlying technologies shaping today's digital world, Taplin—founding director and now director emeritus of the University of Southern California's Annenberg Innovation Lab—is no dummy. He knows that if he asks ordinary internet users whether they hate or love Google or Amazon or Facebook (or whether they'll willingly part with their new iPhones) he's not going to get a lot of buy-in. Even under a hypothetical President Bernie Sanders, regulating Google as a monopoly wouldn't be a meat-and-potatoes issue.

Instead, Taplin creates a counter-narrative in which American technology successes (with the notable exception of Microsoft) represent the kind of rapacious octopus-like capitalism so often caricatured by cartoonists like Thomas Nast. Google and Facebook may not hurt me in particular, but the theory he offers is that they somehow hurt America in the abstract. Taplin essentially reframes American tech success as a retelling of the oil, railroad, banking and telegraph robber-baron trusts of the 19th and early 20th centuries.

But the very tech companies whose success Taplin is absolutely certain is anti-democratic were built on infrastructure and resources that, under federal law and regulation, have been highly regulated throughout his (and my) lifetime. We may disagree about what the regulations should be, but there's little disagreement that there's already a regulatory framework. The regulation of monopoly infrastructures—telephone and telegraph networks, in particular—were what made it possible to refrain from regulating what you said or did on those networks. Regulation at the "wire" level of the infrastructure—and at various technical levels above that—created the space for today's innovative services that provide near-instantaneous access to, potentially, all the information in the world and all the people with whom you would want to stay in touch.

Search engines and other digital tools are, of course, highly disruptive to industries whose traditional model involved having school-age kids hawking ink and wood pulp on street corners. Like Taplin, I still believe newspaper journalism is essential to democracy. Indeed, I read Taplin's op-ed early Sunday morning because I subscribe to the digital edition of the *New York Times*. We must continue to explore new ways to make this necessary journalism not merely survive, but thrive.

But it also bears mentioning that Taplin doesn't mention Craig Newmark or Craigslist in his screed against Google, even though, if you were to buy into the fundamentals of Taplin's argument, Craigslist clearly did more to erode daily newspapers' advertising revenue than Google has ever done. And, yet, at the same time, it's worth noting here that Newmark—like most of the other successful tech moguls Taplin lumps together into a sort of secret-handshake techno-libertarian fraternity—actually gives money to Poynter, ProPublica and other enterprises that actively respond to the very real problem of very fake news.

A little research into the history of scientific discovery puts even the scary Zuckerberg quote about "breaking stuff" in a different light. The philosopher Karl Popper opens his essential book *Conjectures and Refutations*[63] with two quotations: "Experience is the name every one gives to their mistakes," from Oscar Wilde and "Our whole problem is to make the mistakes as fast as possible," from the physicist John Archibald Wheeler.

That sentiment—to be adventurous, to risk things, to learn quickly from making mistakes quickly—is, I believe, exactly what Zuckerberg was getting at. It also extends to making mistakes in our search for a new business model for journalism. But this shouldn't include Jonathan Taplin's great big mistake of looking into the digital future and seeing only places we've been before.

---

63    Karl R. Popper, Conjectures and Refutations: The Growth of Scientific Knowledge (1963).

CHAPTER 7

# Twitter Sucks Because We Suck. Don't Blame @Jack

This article was originally published in *Reason* on July 26, 2018, at
https://reason.com/archives/2018/07/26/twitter-sucks-because-
we-suck-dont-blame.

A lot of criticism of Twitter takes the form of public tweets aimed at
Twitter founder and CEO Jack Dorsey (@jack). Those tweets have
heated up in recent years because Twitter is President Donald Trump's
second-favorite tool for reaching his base. (Perpetual campaign rallies
ranks number one, because of all the cheering.)

These days, many of the complaints charge that Dorsey and his
company aren't doing enough "conversational health work" [64] to make
Twitter an inclusive public forum for divergent opinions that also reduces
or prevents "abusive" speech.

The hard fact is, no matter how much Dorsey commits himself to
making Twitter a safe space for debate, conversation, and entertainment,
he's always going to be criticized for not doing enough. (In this, Dorsey
has the small comfort of not being Mark Zuckerberg, who I'm guessing

---

64   Jack, *A short thread addressing some issues folks are encountering as a result of our
     conversational health work, specifically the perception of shadowbanning based
     on content or ideology. It suffices to say we have a lot more work to do to earn
     peoples trust on how we work.*, Twitter (July 25, 2018), https://twitter.com/jack/
     status/1022196722905296896.

gets orders of magnitude more criticism because Facebook is orders of magnitude more successful—despite today's market slump.) [65] Dorsey will remain in the crosshairs as long as he runs the company—that's because, if you're running a social-media platform, there's no version of top-down censorship of "abusive" content that works out well.

Many of the complaints have focused on whether, under Dorsey's leadership, Twitter is adequately (or consistently) following through on the company's commitment "to help increase the collective health, openness, and civility of public conversation, and to hold ourselves publicly accountable towards progress." Why are the complainers tweeting Dorsey personally? It's partly because Twitter's commitment to the "collective health" of "public conversation" comes from a pinned Tweet on Dorsey's Twitter page. Twitter wants us to understand that the company is devoting more resources to policing its Terms of Service agreement [66] (a.k.a. TOS) that incorporates the "Twitter Rules." [67]

Per the TOS and the Twitter Rules, users are forbidden to use the service for illegal purposes, including active misrepresentation and fraud. They're also officially barred from "abusive behavior," which can include verbal harassment, "unwanted sexual content," and "hateful conduct." That last category warrants its own explanatory page, [68] which provides a nonexclusive list of types of "hateful conduct"—threats, racism, and, if I read it right, pro-genocide content. But Twitter also explains that "context matters": a tweet that might seem like "hateful conduct" considered in itself may in fact be a parody of such content in the context of a larger exchange—or even a direct quote of somebody else, reproduced so it can be analyzed and criticized.

Twitter's policies, taken together, quite properly underscore the fact that human speech and writing are tricky media. Trying to police them simplistically (by banning racist invective, say) can result in the suppression of speech of high social value (like tweets that identify and criticize racist invective). Computer algorithms aren't great at identifying context—we don't yet have I-A.I. (Ironic Artificial Intelligence). And, sadly,

---

65   Josh Constine, *Facebook loses $120 billion in market cap after awful Q2 earnings*, TechCrunch (July 25, 2018), https://techcrunch.com/2018/07/25/fallbook/.

66   *Terms of Service*, Twitter, https://twitter.com/aodespair?lang.

67   *The Twitter Rules*, Twitter Help Center, https://help.twitter.com/en/rules-and-policies/twitter-rules#abusive-behavior.

68   *Hateful Conduct Policy*, Twitter Help Center, https://help.twitter.com/en/rules-and-policies/hateful-conduct-policy.

human beings tasked to respond to complaints about TOS violations aren't always reliable either.

On top of the difficulty of judging (quickly) whether tweets are "abusive," there's also the problem that the judgment is post-hoc. So if you have an active Twitter account, you can post pretty much anything, no matter how offensive or incendiary, with the confidence that it will remain visible to other Twitter users for a while, and perhaps indefinitely. Twitter expressly states in its policies that it relies to a large degree on user complaints to identify content problems in a timely way, but there will always be some policy-violating content that falls through the cracks. At the same time, mischievous users have learned that they can game the complaint system to shut down their tweeting opponents, temporarily or permanently, by reporting them as violating Twitter policies. Neither Twitter nor any other platform has the technology, resources, or personnel to make perfect decisions about whether tweets violate Twitter policies and need to be deleted (or whether users responsible for the tweets in question should be shut down, temporarily or permanently).

Worse, they can't even be relied upon to make consistent decisions. Any content policing of the comprehensive sort that Twitter's most stringent critics call for is certain to lead to censorship that can't be rationally defended. Consider the temporary suspension of the account of the brilliant journalist, TV writer, and producer David Simon, [69] who (now notoriously) has tweeted the wish that certain of his virulent Twitter opponents—many of whom are Trump/MAGA supporter—die of "boils" or a venereal-disease "rash that settles in your lying throat." [70] Simon apparently discovered he'd been suspended when he wanted to tweet something about the death of his friend Anthony Bourdain. [71] Once the suspension was lifted, he learned that some of his tweets had been removed and—of course—wished a plague of boils on Jack Dorsey. "As far as I'm concerned," he wrote, "your standards in this instance are exactly indicative of why social media—and Twitter specifically—is complicit in transforming our national agora into a haven for lies, disinformation, and the politics of totalitarian extremity."

---

69   David Simon, *@AoDespair*, https://twitter.com/aodespair.

70   Emma Stefansky, *David Simon Wishes a Plague of Boils on Jack Dorsey After Twitter Suspension*, Vanity Fair (June 10, 2018), https://www.vanityfair.com/news/2018/06/david-simon-twitter-suspension-jack-dorsey.

71   *Bourdain*, Audacity of Despair (June 8, 2018), https://davidsimon.com/bourdain/.

I asked Simon in a tweet whether he was calling for the more censorship, but just of a different kind. His response?

> You will notice that I have at no point urged Twitter to remove others. Only to preserve the legitimacy of replying to liars, frauds and fascists with a full-throated range of abiding contempt. To require us to engage with such people seriously is to validate the blood libels. [72]

In short, Simon's complaining about inconsistency as well—he believes, not unreasonably, that the best answer for hateful speech is to answer it with contempt.

What this means is, short of having a system in place in which all users' tweets are prescreened by an editor before they become public, we're not going to see any top-down editorial policy—even one informed by complaints from the user community—that works well on the kind of large platform that Twitter is (and that Facebook and other social-media platforms are). Heavy top-down administrative moderation may have worked well enough on the smaller private forums, and on the PC-based bulletin board systems (BBSes) [73] of decades ago. But if the large-scale dominant platforms—not just today's, but tomorrow's as well—are pressured into censoring more and more content, the complexity of identifying what really counts as "abusive" speech guarantees that some large fraction of the user population will be unhappy with the results.

The platform companies know this. They're (mostly) quite aware that Section 230 of the Communications Decency Act [74] (including its most recent amended version [75]) gives them the right to curate user content. They're also painfully aware that invoking that right leads both to higher expectations of editorial control and to more and more dissatisfaction [76]

---

72  David Simon, *You will notice that I have at no point urged Twitter to remove others. Only to preserve the legitimacy of replying to liars, frauds and fascists with a full-throated range of abiding contempt. To require us to engage with such people seriously is to validate the blood libels.*, Twitter (June 22, 2018), https://twitter.com/aodespair/status/1010368062351183872.

73  *Bulletin board system*, Wikipedia (last edited Dec. 11, 2018), https://en.wikipedia.org/wiki/Bulletin˙board˙system.

74  47 U.S.C. § 230.

75  Allow States and Victims to Fight Online Sex Trafficking Act of 2017, Pub. L. No. 115-164, 132 Stat. 1253.

76  jack, *supra* note 1.

as users disagree with particular editorial decisions. Even so, Twitter, like all the other dominant platforms, is investing more in finding ways to reduce user complaints about abusive content. But until we have built our Ironic A.I., the best fix is still to remind users they can make their own decisions about what to say and what to hear.

# CHAPTER 8

# Tech People Are the Last People I Would Trust to Regulate Speech

This article was originally published in *Slate* on October 19, 2018, at https://slate.com/technology/2018/10/david-simon-twitter-ban-mike-godwin-interview.html. It comprises an interview with David Simon.

The minute after I watched the first episode of *The Wire*, I found myself asking: Is this the best show ever to be on television? (It was.) So of course I've followed David Simon's work through his post–Hurricane Katrina New Orleans series Treme and later his '70s-porn-era New York City drama *The Deuce*. Like me, Simon once paid his rent primarily as a journalist, but he leveraged his newspaper years into creating TV drama that, if anything, was as good as (or maybe better than) the best journalism I'd seen until then—capturing crime and social problems with a consistent recognition that our real-life heroes, like our real-life villains, have a gift for being their own worst enemies.

On Twitter, Simon has won a unique reputation as a prolific hurler of baroque insults targeting those he believes are poisoning the social media platform. After the 2016 election, people in my feed would tag me regarding Simon's tweets comparing both Twitter trolls and genuinely monstrous people like Syria's President Bashar al-Assad to Hitler, Nazis, fascists, and the like. Some clearly hoped that, as the creator of Godwin's law, I might render a verdict against him as a Godwin's lawbreaker, but I had already written that informed, knowledgeable Nazi comparisons[77] won't earn my criticism. At its best, I saw Simon's frequently colorful exercise of his First Amendment rights as high-quality performance art.

Twitter's management took a different view and has suspended Simon[78] twice this year so far for his invective, some of which is aimed at Twitter's masters.[79] When he came back for the second time, I asked him whether he'd be willing to be interviewed about Twitter and social media generally. He quickly agreed, and after a phone call working out the details, we began this interview in Twitter's direct messages, shifting midway to email. Our exchanges ranged from talk about what Twitter is doing wrong to larger social ills that seem to be undermining American democracy. This transcript has been lightly edited and condensed.

Mike Godwin: *You've relished using Twitter to challenge trolls and racists and other objectionable tweeters, only to get suspended—"sent to Twitter jail"—more than once. You've quit Twitter, but now you're back. Can this relationship be saved?*

David Simon: Not much of a relationship, I gotta say. There is no human intellect with which to engage, just the Great Algorando [Simon's word[80] for the mystery personnel superintending Twitter's algorithmic search for policy-violating tweets] in the Twitter basement, which is an epic fail in terms of creating any ethical paradigm that anyone should respect. Twitter has no answer to being a repository for all manner of libel, intolerance, and organized disinformation. Nor do they seek an answer. It is a platform that thrives on today's open warfare between fact and falsehood. Instead, they police decorum. How does anyone

---

77    Mike Godwin, *Sure, call Trump a Nazi. Just make sure you know what youre talking about,* Wash. Post (May 15, 2018), https://www.washingtonpost.com/posteverything/wp/2015/12/14/sure-call-trump-a-nazi-just-make-sure-you-know-what-youre-talking-about/.

78    Mike Godwin, *Twitter Sucks Because We Suck. Don't Blame @Jack,* Reason.com (July 26, 2018), https://reason.com/archives/2018/07/26/twitter-sucks-because-we-suck-dont-blame.

79    Michael Roffman et al., *The Wire creator David Simon suspended from Twitter after bashing Trump supporters,* Consequence Of Sound (June 11, 2018), https://consequenceofsound.net/2018/06/david-simon-twitter-ban/.

80    David Simon, *Oh. To the submorons manning the Great Algorando at Tweet Central: What scans here is an anti-aircraft missile aimed upasswards of an inanimate balloon. The imagined outcome is for no physical harm to a lying shitcrisp beneath said balloon, who suffers only a drycleaning bill.,* Twitter (Sept. 24, 2018), https://twitter.com/aodespair/status/1044174931846746113.

seriously engage with that? And with regard to my own experiences, I certainly doubt CEO Jack Dorsey or anyone capable of voicing his logic is going to get on the phone or fire off emails in order to muster a coherent explanation. I'm not holding my breath, anyway.

Godwin: *You've written that Twitter can't just bail on the issue of content and let the whole public forum be poisoned by bad speech, but you've also said you're a strong First Amendment/free speech guy. How do you square these two ideas?*

Simon: I can't conjure a social media platform moving at the speed of Twitter—with the limited human resources that they are willing to support on their current profit margins—that can actually regulate and police disinformation, libel, and harassment. Not well, anyway. To do that job, they're going to need—dare I say it—some trained journalists. Editors, by name. Fact-checking is labor-intensive, and it's skilled labor. So it isn't happening—not in the near future, not for the most fundamental responsibility of any media site: policing disinformation and preserving accuracy. So, OK. It's going to be a free-for-all, and the lies and affronts will be across the internet before the truth gets its boots on. That's the given.

But if that is, in fact, the given, then the last thing that Twitter should be doing is policing decorum, or trying to leach hostility from the platform. Why? Because the appropriate response to overt racism, to anti-Semitism, to libel, to organized disinformation campaigns is not to politely reason with such in long threads of fact-sharing. All that does is lend a fundamental credence to the worst kind of speech—which, grievously, seems to be the paradigm that Twitter prefers at present. It's a paradigm that offers two basic choices: Ignore the deplorati—which allows the dishonesty or cruelty to stand in public view and acquire the veneer of credibility by doing so. Or worse, engage in some measure of serious disputation with all manner of horseshit, which also grants trash the veneer of credibility. In 1935, the reply to Streicher[81] or Goebbels[82] quoting The Protocols of the Elders of Zion and asserting that Jews drink the blood of baptized Christian babies is not to begin arguing that "no, Jews do not drink Christian baby blood" and deliver a long explanation of The Protocols as a czarist forgery in chapter and verse. The correct response is to call Julius Streicher a submoronic piece

---

81  *Julius Streicher: Biography*, Holocaust Encyclopedia, https://encyclopedia.ushmm. org/content/en/article/julius-streicher-biography.

82  *Joseph Goebbels*, Wikipedia (last edited Jan. 25, 2019), https://en.wikipedia.org/ wiki/Joseph Goebbels.

of shit, marking him as such for the rest of the sentient, and move on to some more meaningful exchange of ideas. So it is with Twitter. If I'm gonna exist there, I'm not going to let the most rancid shit stand on my feed as if it's plausible, but nor am I going to treat it as deserving of serious argument. I'm gonna call it out quickly and block—and do so with as much flair and performance as I can so at least the process won't be boring. But effectively, what I am doing is marking the [land mines] for the rest of the platoon to block as well. It's a permanent, quotidian task—but given that Twitter is not going to become a responsible news organization that fact-checks the commentary and regulates it on that basis, what else can we do?

Godwin: *I agree that human beings are better than algorithms (at least for now), but there's lots of evidence that human beings screw up these curation issues, too, isn't there? Even if Twitter staffed up with people (even journalists!) to respond to complaints about terms of service violations, wouldn't there still be complaints about bias and unfairness?*

Simon: As there always are—even in the most consistently edited media and on the most carefully regulated platforms. Everyone is arguing about what gets play on the *New York Times* op-ed [page], or in the Letters column. But I'd rather take my chance arguing with and defending myself to a sentient human than being arbitrarily tagged by a flat-brained algorithm. If you are going to police your site, then make the effort to at least entertain an appellate process that helps you establish the basic context to proceed with banning people or censoring opinion. To this moment, having been banned twice for comic hyperbole, I've not had either a written reply to my appeal of the absurdity or a conversation with any living soul at Twitter.

In fact, the cheese-eating mooks actually took down one of the tweets unilaterally without ever engaging me. I wouldn't delete the tweet, and they would not return me to the platform until I did. So, OK, fair enough. I was willing to quit and just leave the thing up there as evidence that it was neither harassment nor threat. But no, rather than engage on the merits, they quietly deleted the tweet after several weeks while leaving the form demanding that I do so on my account. Someone alerted me that it was gone, and after checking repeatedly and seeing as much, I finally deleted what wasn't there, if only to tell Jack Dorsey once again that he deserves boils.

Why are they not honing a process by which they might address the excesses of their algorithmic interventions? Or defend those interventions?

Because they're not good at this stuff. And their programmatic response sucks. And if they have to explain themselves in a cohesive and thoughtful way, they're going to fall on their ass. They can't explain it in detail—as it is actually applied on a case-by-case basis—so they won't. On the ethics of all this, Twitter is a fucking mess.

Godwin: *Twitter gets savaged for hosting obvious trolls, but since the elections of 2016, Facebook has been taking a lot of heat for so-called filter bubbles, echo chambers that intensify extreme opinions, plus its news feed, on the theory that the algorithmically picked news sources push you toward extremes. But Facebook's de-emphasizing the news feed has forced news sources that rely on internet advertising, like Slate, to take a hit.* [83]

Simon: I barely use Facebook, and only then for my private connections with friends and family. I'm there under an assumed name. And I'm actually less of a student of and participant in that particular agora. Fact is, after years of resisting it and seeing it as a flawed vehicle for arguing or discussing anything seriously, I got on Twitter as a means of promoting my television programming and, occasionally, some bit of prose work on my blog. Or of highlighting other content that I thought had merit. It was in the last election cycle that I began to realize, to my chagrin, that public rhetoric is now arriving at light speed on these social platforms. They are already in effect the first news cycle, and with regard to the worst kind of spin and rumor, there is often scarcely a second news cycle in which facts ever catch up. Or so it seems.

So I've been drawn into the national argument where it seems to begin. But again, it's a corrupted platform. If you can't sever the bots and professional trolls and find a decent argument with someone else who is really wrestling with stuff, then to what purpose? The best you can do with a troll or bot is use them in the same fashion that Edgar Bergen [84] used Charlie McCarthy—as a rhetorical prop. If you tell me that Facebook is any different, then maybe I should dump Twitter and die on the other hill. But either way, the idea that all of these platforms are subject to political manipulations and agitprop is, by now, obvious. There are no gatekeepers. There is no commitment to police for accuracy. The

83  Will Oremus, *A Close Look at How Facebook's Retreat From the News Has Hurt One Particular Website—Ours,* Slate (June 27, 2018), https://slate.com/technology/2018/06/facebooks-retreat-from-the-news-has-painful-for-publishers-including-slate.html.

84  *Edgar Bergen,* Wikipedia (last edited Feb. 3, 2019), https://en.wikipedia.org/wiki/Edgar Bergen.

metadata delivered by users can be repurposed into political weaponry by interested parties. And they have no viable institutional response to these realities.

It's as if they can't solve murders, robberies, and rapes in this town, so rather than confront the long and hard journey of real police work, the folks at Twitter are going to make this the least-jaywalkingest ville in Christendom.

But to be clear, I have no interest in encouraging anyone in any authoritative capacity to ban speech on a platform that has become de facto part of our national agora. And given how miserable Twitter has thus far proved itself at being capable of discerning even sarcasm or comic hyperbole, and how tolerant it is as a platform for the overt and organized slander and libel of individuals and cohorts, tech people are in fact the last people I would trust to regulate speech.

[At this point, Simon and I both realized we were getting more essayistic—so we migrated to email.]

Godwin: *I want to come back to the idea of employing more journalists, more editors—especially since those jobs are scarce. It's great if more reporters and editors are working, but doesn't the whole idea of social media, the whole success of it, spring from "disintermediation"? From being able to step up and say something to the public without having to get an editor's approval? The way we talked about the internet in the early days—not just social media but the internet itself—was that it opened the door for everyone to speak to large audiences. That said, it was obvious from the outset that some high percentage of the speakers was going to end up being dopes. Or worse.*

Simon: If I had possession over Judgment Day and the resources of Twitter, here is what I would do:

I would not throw open my review process to fretting about name-calling or comic hyperbole or even exchanges of abject contempt and disgust because, as we all know, there is plenty on the platform that deserves a hailstorm of contempt and disgust. Instead, I would use my limited resources to open the gates to complaints about intellectual frauds, libels, and disinformation campaigns. And I would empower Twitter users to be, if not the ultimate arbiters of these issues, to be a force, in a fundamental way, that begins to self-police the site.

How? Same way as users now report what they perceive to be "offensive" content, I would demand that they raise their game and raise the stakes to reporting that which can be empirically demonstrated to be false. There's your disintermediation. The users themselves deliver complaints that go to the heart of Twitter's fundamental weakness: This is a libel. That is a lie. Let them call it out and deliver the empirical proof. Let them be the police and then have Twitter—in conjunction with some in-house research equivalent of Snopes or some other fact-checking forum—be the court of jurisdiction for claims that originate with Twitter users themselves. That limits Twitter's responsibility to only the fact-checking that is requested organically by users, not extending its responsibility over the whole of the content. It also makes it imperative for objecting users to bring intellectual and journalistic rigor to their complaints, further girding the process. And it creates a standard that makes it possible for Twitter to remove those who can be evidenced to be not merely in error about facts, but purposefully and repeatedly employing libel and disinformation.

And here is the stick I would employ:

If it can be demonstrated that a user's content is subjective, well, that is a function of rhetoric and beyond any sanction.

If it can be demonstrated that a user's content is empirically false, but there is no evidence of an intent to mislead or libel, then a request to remove the falsehood could be undertaken and the user could be given the choice of removing the tweet or self-correcting publicly.

If it can be demonstrated that a user's content is part of a continuing and persistent pattern of employing disinformation, fraud, or libel, then the account can be suspended.

Isn't this a more fundamental use of limited journalistic resources than to stop David Simon from telling some racist troll he ought to consider succumbing to a nonlethal skin disorder? And if Snopes can do this as an online resource, how the fuck is it so elusive for Twitter?

Godwin: *Snopes sometimes seems to be limping along*[85] *as a nonprofit based on donations (maybe some big donations from the companies, like $100,000 from Facebook*[86] *in 2017, but not too big). But subsidizing Snopes seems like something that would be well within even Twitter's uncertain profitability.*

Simon: Great to hear. Let them do it. Immediately. Just [recently] James fucking Woods showed up on Twitter to once again declare George

---

85  Daniel Victor, *Snopes, in Heated Legal Battle, Asks Readers for Money to Survive*, N.Y. Times (July 24, 2017), https://www.nytimes.com/2017/07/24/business/media/snopes-crowdfunding-proper-media.html.

86  *Disclosures*, Snopes.com, https://www.snopes.com/disclosures/.

Soros to be a Nazi collaborator.[87] Never mind that Snopes has thoroughly and impartially dismissed this claim—Woods[88] is still rambling around on the platform repeating the big lie. Wouldn't it be great if an in-house component simply flagged that tweet, alerted the bitter little fuckmook as to its fraudulence and gave him the opportunity to remove it himself or, even better, asked him to post a corrective and apologize like a grown-ass human? And when he fails, suspend his libelous account. Now there is an actual deterrent to using Twitter for organized libel and disinformation.

Godwin: *I'll give you a couple of examples where I think the social media platforms have done good in a way that traditional media never have managed to do (although there's been some symbiosis here). The first is #MeToo. It's suddenly become possible for many more women's voices to be heard. (And those of men too—as with Kevin Spacey.)*

*The second is #BlackLivesMatter. Everybody who knew anything about policing and criminal law, both in cities and in small-town and rural environments, knew that people of color were more at risk in encounters with police. But now, all of a sudden, we can abruptly publicize police violence, or even explosions of insane verbal racism. Isn't the radical empowerment of individuals who need it some kind of a balance for all the dumbass things other Twitter twits do?*

Simon: Indeed. And you're arguing in some of this for the power that exists in the ubiquity of the smartphone, with its instantaneous video capability. No disputing that revolution, and it is overwhelmingly for the better to have first-generation evidence of what is occurring with regard to authoritarian action or to off-the-cuff remarks or affronts by people. Sure.

But be careful about claiming that unfettered access by anonymous complainants to social media platforms has done a singular service to the real work of #BlackLivesMatter or #MeToo. With #MeToo in particular, I would argue that traditional journalism—with its elaborate construct for proving accusations, documenting patterns of behavior, and confronting offenders and knocking down their false counterclaims is what delivered Weinstein, Moonves, Toback, Cosby, and others. Yes, the

---

87    James Woods, *The degree to which this one Nazi collaborator has undermined the stability of Western democracies is virtually incalculable. He is satanic.*, Twitter (Oct. 13, 2018), https://twitter.com/realjameswoods/status/1051126299526385664.

88    David Emery, *FACT CHECK: Was George Soros an SS Officer or Nazi Collaborator During World War II?*, Snopes.com (Feb. 4, 2018), https://www.snopes.com/fact-check/george-soros-ss-nazi-germany/.

initial spark may be a bubbling of complaint—some on the record, but much of it anonymous—on social media. But then the rigor of journalistic investigation establishes the credibility of the narrative. What the *New Yorker* and the *New York Times* did with Weinstein was magnificent, and it was definitive in a way that the rumored rage of social media can never be. They worked the claims and confirmed and published the totality of the story. And there was a totality.

Regrettably, I can point to some case studies in which the level of accusation, even if we credit the claims for what they are, actually does a disservice to #MeToo by flattening all allegation—however important or however modest—into the same claimed affront.

Same thing with Black Lives Matter. We have reached a point where every act of police violence or every filmed police shooting has its turn on social media. This is for the better. But we have also reached a point where it's clear that every act of police violence or every police shooting is not unjustifiable. Often, law officers are heedless, brutal, indifferent, and even sadistic. That is now rightfully grist for new media, and as a result it is an issue being highlighted for address by old media. Sometimes, the police are in a fight not of their choosing, in which case it is not police brutality if the cops win the fight. In Baltimore, we just went through that pregnant social media pause when city police, who have all kinds of deserved credibility issues, said they shot someone who was shooting at them. The rumor mill began to churn a bit until the department released the video. And yes, this time the police were returning fire[89] in a running gun battle with one of the pursuing officers wounded.

Point being that no one sentient doesn't see the value in all of this first-generation video content now being delivered. And social media is the delivery platform, to be sure. But what comes behind the delivery of that material still matters as much as it ever did: Particularly when you become aware of how even video content can be manipulated, edited, deconstructed by interested parties. I am as exhilarated as anyone by the digital revolution and what it allows ordinary people to acquire of the world and deliver with immediacy. But I am also intent on what an impartial, professional journalist acquires when he corroborates the video and contextualizes the video.

---

89   Christina Tkacik et al., *Baltimore police officer wounded, man killed in shootout in block that's seen recent spate of violence*, Baltimoresun.com (Sept. 24, 2018), https://www.baltimoresun.com/news/maryland/crime/bs-md-ci-officer-shot-20180923-story.html.

Godwin: *I like the idea that users themselves can be, and are, more empowered to answer false facts and raise questions about fake news—supplementing or complementing the traditional press. But Twitter and Facebook in particular are feeling pressured to "do something." Often by governments. Many conservatives are absolutely certain that the platforms are biased against them and are censoring them. Progressive activists are equally certain that they're the targets of censorship. After Brexit and the election of President Trump, the governments around the world are looking for someone easy to blame for the weird political moment we're in. Internet platforms are new, so they're an easy target. The way TV used to be. And movies and radio before that.*

Simon: OK. I don't dispute that Twitter and other such platforms are being bashed from all points of the political compass. Same for old media for all of its history. That goes with the job.

I'm saying they have responded by doing the wrong fucking something. They are responding in such a way that they are, in effect, normalizing the worst kind of organized disinformation and hate speech. They have set up a both-sides construct that is disturbingly reminiscent of the Trumpian reaction to Charlottesville.

It's a kind of abdication.

# CHAPTER 9

# Everything That's Wrong with Social Media and Big Internet Companies

## *Part 1*

This article was originally published in *Techdirt* on November 29, 2017, at https://www.techdirt.com/articles/20171128/23565738694/everything-thats-wrong-with-social-media-big-internet-companies-part-1.shtml.

Some of today's anxiety about social-media platforms is driven by the concern that Russian operatives somehow used Facebook and Twitter to affect our electoral process. Some of it's due a general perception that big American social-media companies, amorally or immorally driven by the profit motive, are eroding our privacy and selling our data to other companies or turning it over to the government—or both. Some of it's due to the perception that Facebook, Twitter, Instagram, and other platforms are bad for us—that maybe even Google's or Microsoft's search engines are bad for us [90]—and that they make us worse people or debase public

---

90   Nicholas Carr, The Shallows: What the Internet Is Doing to Our Brains (2010).

discourse. Taken together, it's more than enough fodder for politicians[91] or would-be pundits[92] to stir up generalized anxiety about big tech.

But regardless of where this moral panic[93] came from, the current wave of anxiety about internet intermediaries and social-media platforms has its own momentum now. So we can expect many more calls for regulation of these internet tools and platforms in the coming months and years. Which is why it's a good idea to itemize the criticisms we've already seen, or are likely to see, in current and future public-policy debates about regulating the internet. We need to chart the kinds of arguments for new internet regulation that are going to confront us, so I've been compiling a list of them. It's a work in progress, but here are three major claims that are driving recent expressions of concern about social media and internet companies generally.[94]

**(1) Social media are bad for you because they use algorithms to target you, based on the data they collect about you.** It's well-understood now that Facebook and other platforms gather data about what interests you in order to shape what kinds of advertising you see and what kind of news stories you see in your news feed (if you're using a service that provides one). Some part of the anxiety here is driven by the idea (more or less correct) that an internet company is gathering data about your likes, dislikes, interests, and usage patterns, which means it knows more about you in some ways than perhaps your friends (on social media and in what we now quaintly call "real life") know about you. Possibly more worrying than that, the companies are using algorithms—computerized procedures aimed at analyzing and interpreting data—to decide what ads and topics to show you.

It's worth noting, however, that commercial interests have been gathering data about you since long before the advent of the internet.

91   Ted Johnson, *Senators Blast Tech Giants: I Dont Think You Get It on Russian Influence*, Variety (Nov. 1, 2017), https://variety.com/2017/politics/news/dianne-feinstein-facebook-russian-influence-1202604269/.

92   Elizabeth Kolbert, *Who Owns the Internet?*, N.Y.er (Aug. 21, 2017), https://www.newyorker.com/magazine/2017/08/28/who-owns-the-internet.

93   *Moral panic*, Wikipedia (last edited Jan. 27, 2019), https://en.wikipedia.org/wiki/Moral panic.

94   Tony Romm, *Sen. Al Franken torched Amazon, Facebook and Google for using their algorithms to maintain their reach*, Recode (Nov. 8, 2017), https://www.recode.net/2017/11/8/16624714/al-franken-amazon-facebook-google-russia.

In the 1980s and before in the United States, if you joined one book club or ordered one winter coat on Land's End, you almost certainly ended up on mailing lists and received other offers and many, many mail-order catalogs. Your transactional information was marketed, packaged, and sold to other vendors (as was your payment and credit history). If false information was shared about you, you perhaps had some options ranging from writing remove-me-from-your-list letters to legal remedies under the federal Fair Credit Reporting Act.[95] But the process was typically cumbersome, slow, and less-than-completely satisfactory (and still is when it comes to credit-bureau records). One advantage with some internet platforms is that (a) they give you options to quit seeing ads you don't like (and often to say just why you don't like them), and (b) the internet companies, anxious about regulation, don't exactly want to piss you off. (In that sense, they may be more responsive than TiVo[96] could be.)

Of course it's fair—and, I think, prudent—to note that the combination of algorithms and "big data" may have real consequences for democracy and for freedom of speech. Yale's Jack Balkin has recently written an excellent law-review article that targets these issues.[97] At the same time, it seems possible for internet platforms to anonymize data they collect in ways that pre-internet commercial enterprises never could.

**(2) Social Media are bad for you because they allow you to create a filter bubble[98] where you see only (or mostly) opinions you agree with. (2)(a) Social media are bad for you because they foment heated arguments between you and those you disagree with.** To some extent, these two arguments run against each other—if you only hang out online with people who think like you, it seems unlikely that you'll have quite so many fierce arguments, right? (But maybe the arguments between people who share most opinions and backgrounds are fiercer?) In any case, it seems clear that both "filter bubbles" and "flames" can occur. But

---

95  Fair Credit Reporting Act, 15 U.S.C. § 1681.

96  Peter Duke, *My TiVo thinks I'm Gay,* YouTube (Sept. 9, 2008), https://www.youtube.com/watch?v=PoUJvAQg7KI.

97  Jack M. Balkin, *Free Speech in the Algorithmic Society: Big Data, Private Governance, and New School Speech Regulation,* 51 UC Davis L. Rev. 1149 (2018), https://lawreview.law.ucdavis.edu/issues/51/3/Essays/51-3˙Balkin.pdf.

98  *Filter bubble,* Wikipedia (last edited Jan. 24, 2019), https://en.wikipedia.org/wiki/Filter˙bubble.

when they do, statistical research suggests, it's primarily because of user choice, not algorithms. In fact, as a study in Public Opinion Quarterly reported last year, [99] the algorithmically driven social-media platforms may be both increasing polarization and increasing users' exposures to opposing views. The authors summarize their conclusions this way:

> We find that social networks and search engines are associated with an increase in the mean ideological distance between individuals. However, somewhat counterintuitively, these same channels also are associated with an increase in an individual's exposure to material from his or her less preferred side of the political spectrum.

In contrast, the case that "filter bubbles" are a particular, polarizing problem relies to a large degree not on statistics but on anecdotal evidence. [100] That is, the people who don't like arguing or who can't bear too different a set of political opinions tend to curate their social-media feeds accordingly, while people who don't mind arguments (or even love them) have no difficulty encountering heterodox viewpoints on Facebook or Twitter. (At various times I've fallen into one or the other category on the internet, even before the invention of social media or the rise of Google's search engine. [101])

The argument about "filter bubbles"—people self-segregating and self-isolating into like-minded online groups—is an argument that predates modern social media and the dominance of modern search engines. Law professor Cass Sunstein advanced it in his 2001 book, *Republic.com* [102] and hosted a website forum to promote that book. I remember this well because I showed up in the forum to express my disagreement with his conclusions—hoping that my showing up as a dissenter would itself raise questions about Sunstein's version of the

99   Seth Flaxman et al., *Filter Bubbles, Echo Chambers, and Online News Consumption*, 80 Pub. Opinion Q. 298 (2016), https://academic.oup.com/poq/article-abstract/80/S1/298/2223402.

100   William H. Dutton, *Fake news, echo chambers and filter bubbles: Underresearched and overhyped*, The Conversation (May 5, 2017), http://theconversation.com/fake-news-echo-chambers-and-filter-bubbles-underresearched-and-over-hyped-76688.

101   Mike Godwin, *Trashing the flamers*, Salon.com (May 15, 1998), https://www.salon.com/1998/05/15/feature˙319/.

102   Cass R. Sunstein, Republic.com (2001).

"filter bubble" hypothesis. I didn't imagine I'd change Sunstein's mind, though, so I was unsurprised to see the professor has revised and refined his hypothesis, first in *Republic.com 2.0*[103] in 2007 and now in *#Republic: Divided Democracy in the Age of Social Media,*[104] published just this year.

**(3) Social media are bad for you because they are profit-centered, mostly (including the social media that don't generate profits).** "If you're not paying for the product, you're the product."[105] That's a maxim with real memetic resonance,[106] I have to admit. This argument is related to argument number 1 above, except that instead of focusing on one's privacy concerns, it's aimed at the even-more-disturbing idea that we're being commodified and sold by the companies who give us free services. This necessarily includes Google and Facebook, which provide users with free access but which gather data that is used primarily to target ads. Both of those companies are profitable. Twitter, which also serves ads to its users, isn't yet profitable, but of course aspires to be.[107]

As a former employee of the Wikimedia Foundation—which is dedicated to providing Wikipedia and other informational resources to everyone in the world, for free—I don't quite know what to make of this. Certainly the accounts of the early days of Google[108] or of Facebook[109] suggest that advertising as a mission typically arose after the founders realized that their new internet services needed to make money. But once any new company starts making money by the yacht-load, it's easy to dismiss the whole enterprise as essentially mercenary.

---

103    Cass R. Sunstein, Republic.com 2.0 (2007).

104    Cass R. Sunstein, #Republic: Divided Democracy in the Age of Social Media (2017).

105    Mike Masnick, *Stop Saying "If You're Not Paying, You're the Product"*, Techdirt (Dec. 20, 2012) [hereinafter Masnick, *You're the Product*], https://www.techdirt.com/articles/20121219/18272921446/stop-saying-if-youre-not-paying-youre-product.shtml.

106    Mike Godwin, *Meme, Counter-meme*, Wired (Oct. 1, 1994), https://www.wired.com/1994/10/godwin-if-2/.

107    Pia Gadkari, *How does Twitter make money?*, BBC News (Nov. 7, 2013), https://www.bbc.com/news/business-24397472.

108    Steven Levy, In The Plex: How Google Thinks, Works, and Shapes Our Lives (2011).

109    Ben Mezrich, The Accidental Billionaires: The Founding of Facebook: A Tale of Sex, Money, Genius and Betrayal (2010).

(In Europe, much more ambivalent to commercial enterprises than the United States, it's far more common to encounter this dismissiveness. This helps explain some the Europe's greater willingness to regulate the online world.[110] The fact that so many successful internet companies are American also helps explain that impulse.[111])

But Wikipedia has steadfastly resisted even the temptation to sell ads—even though it could have become an internet commercial success just as IMDB.com has—because the Wikipedia volunteers and the Wikimedia Foundation see value in providing something useful and fun to everyone regardless of whether one gets rich doing so. So do the creators of free and open-source software.[112] If creating free products and services doesn't always mean you're out to sell other people into data slavery, shouldn't we at least consider the possibility that social-media companies may really mean it when they declare their intentions to do well by doing good? ("Do Well By Doing Good" is a maxim commonly attributed to Benjamin Franklin—who of course sold advertising, and even wrote advertising copy, for his *Pennsylvania Gazette*.[113]) I think it's a good idea to follow Mike Masnick's advice to stop repeating this "you're the product" slogan[114]—unless you're ready to condemn all traditional journals that subsidize giving their content to you through advertising.

So that's the current top three chart-toppers for the Social Media-Are-Bad-For-You Greatest Hits. But this is a crowded field—only the tip of the iceberg when it comes to trendy criticisms of social-media platforms, search engines, and unregulated mischievous speech on the internet—and we expect to see many other competing criticisms of Facebook, Twitter, Google, etc. surface in the weeks and months to come.

---

110   European Comm'n, *Digital Single Market date,* https://ec.europa.eu/digital-single-market/en/online-platforms-digital-single-market.

111   *Europe's best days on the internet could lie ahead,* Fin. Times (Jan. 1, 2015), https://www.ft.com/content/3da2fe12-844f-11e4-bae9-00144feabdc0.

112   *Free and open-source software,* Wikipedia (last edited Feb. 3, 2019), https://en.wikipedia.org/wiki/Free˙and˙open-source˙software.

113   Am. Adver. Fed'n, *Benjamin Franklin,* Advert. Hall Fame, http://advertisinghall.org/members/member˙bio.php?memid=632.

114   Masnick, *You're the Product, supra* note 16.

# CHAPTER 10

# Everything That's Wrong with Social Media and Big Internet Companies:

## *Part 2*

This article was originally published in *Techdirt* on January 30, 2018, at https://www.techdirt.com/articles/20180128/11001839096/ everything-thats-wrong-with-social-media-big-internet-companies-part-2.shtml.

This Part should have come earlier; Part 1 was published in November. I'd hubristically imagined that this is a project that might take a week or a month. But I didn't take into account the speed with which the landscape of the criticism is changing. For example, just as you're trying to do more research into whether Google really is making us dumber,[115] another pundit (Farhad Manjoo at the *New York Times*) comes along and argues that Apple—a tech giant no less driven by commercial motives than Google and its parent company, Alphabet—ought to redesign its products[116] to make us smarter (by making them less addictive). That

---

115   Carr, *supra.*

116   Farhad Manjoo, *Its Time for Apple to Build a Less Addictive iPhone*, N.Y. Times (Jan. 17, 2018), https://www.nytimes.com/2018/01/17/technology/apple-addiction-iphone.html.

is, it's Apple's job to save us from Gmail, Facebook, Twitter, Instagram, and other attention-demanding internet media—which we connect to through Apple's products, as well as many others.

In these same few weeks, Facebook has announced it's retooling[117] the user experience for Facebook users in ways aimed at making the experience more personal and interactive and less passive. Is this an implicit admission that Facebook, up until now, has been bad for us? If so, is it responding to the charges that many observers have leveled at social-media companies—that they're bad for us and that they're bad for democracy.

And only this last week, social-media companies have responded to concerns[118] about political extremists (foreign and domestic) in Senate testimony. Although the senators had broad concerns (ISIS recruitment, bomb-making information on YouTube), there was, of course, some allocation of time on the ever-present question of Russian "misinformation campaigns,"[119] which may not have altered the outcome of 2016's elections but still may aim to affect 2018 mid-terms and beyond.

These are recent developments, but coloring them all is a more generalized social anxiety about social media and big internet companies that is nowhere better summarized than in Senator Al Franken's last major public policy address.[120] Whatever you think of Senator Franken's tenure, I think his speech was a useful accumulation of the growing sentiment among commentators that there's something out of control[121] with social media and internet companies that needs to be brought back into control.

---

117   Mike Masnick, *Media Freaks Out About Facebook Changes; Maybe They Shouldn't Have Become So Reliant On Facebook,* Techdirt (Jan. 16, 2018), https://www.techdirt.com/articles/20180113/11333938996/media-freaks-out-about-facebook-changes-maybe-they-shouldnt-have-become-so-reliant-facebook.shtml.

118   Ali Breland, *Facebook, Twitter, YouTube detail fight against extremists at Senate hearing,* The Hill (Jan. 17, 2018), https://thehill.com/policy/technology/369378-facebook-twitter-and-youtube-detail-fight-against-extremists-during-senate.

119   Colin Lecher, *Facebook, YouTube, and Twitter were grilled by lawmakers about terrorist content on social media,* The Verge (Jan. 17, 2018), https://www.theverge.com/2018/1/17/16900858/facebook-youtube-twitter-terrorism-senate-hearing.

120   Al Franken, *We must not let Big Tech threaten our security, freedoms and democracy,* The Guardian (Nov. 8, 2017), https://www.theguardian.com/commentisfree/2017/nov/08/big-tech-security-freedoms-democracy-al-franken.

121   Nitasha Tiku, *Al Franken Just Gave the Speech Big Tech Has Been Dreading,* Wired (Nov. 9, 2017), https://www.wired.com/story/al-franken-just-gave-the-speech-big-tech-has-been-dreading/.

Now, let's be clear: even if I'm skeptical here about some claims that social media and internet giants are bad for us, that doesn't mean these criticisms necessarily lack any merit at all. But it's always worth remembering that, historically, every new mass medium (and mass-medium platform) has been declared first to be wonderful for us, and then to be terrible for us. So it's always important to ask whether any particular claim about the harms of social media or internet companies is reactive, reflexive . . . or whether it's grounded in hard facts.

Here are reasons 4, 5, and 6 to believe social media are bad for us.

**(4) Social media (and maybe some other internet services) are bad for us because they're super-addictive, especially on our sweet, slick handheld devices.** "It's Time for Apple to Build a Less Addictive iPhone," according to *New York Times* tech columnist Farhad Manjoo, who published a column to that effect recently. To be sure, although "Addictive" is in the headline, Manjoo is careful to say upfront that, although iPhone use may leave you feeling "enslaved," it's not "not Apple's fault" and it "isn't the same as [the addictiveness] of drugs or alcohol." Manjoo's column was inspired by an open letter from an ad-hoc [122] advocacy group [123] that included an investment-management firm and the California State Teachers Retirement System (both of which are Apple shareholders). The letter, available at ThinkDifferentlyAboutKids.com [124] calls for Apple to add more parental-control choices for its iPhones (and other internet-connected devices, one infers). After consulting with experts, the letter's signatories argue, "we note that Apple's current limited set of parental controls in fact dictate a more binary, all or nothing approach, with parental options limited largely to shutting down or allowing full access to various tools and functions." Per the letter's authors: "we have reviewed the evidence and we believe there is a clear need for Apple to offer parents more choices and tools to help them ensure that young consumers are using your products in an optimal manner."

---

122   Glyn Moody, *Shareholder Groups Say Apple Should Do More To Address Gadget "Addiction" Among Young People: Should It?*, Techdirt (Jan. 11, 2018), https://www.techdirt.com/articles/20180109/05152038966/shareholder-groups-say-apple-should-do-more-to-address-gadget-addiction-among-young-people-should-it.shtml.

123   *Id.*

124   The original website no longer appears to be active, but the letter is also available here: *Open Letter from JANA Partners and CALSTRS to APPLE INC* (Jan. 6, 2018), https://imgur.com/gallery/Afgem0C.

Why Apple in particular? Obviously, the fact that two of the signatories own a couple of billion dollars' worth of Apple stock explains this choice to some extent. But one hard fact is that Apple's share of the smartphone market mostly stays in the 12-to-20-percent range. [125] (Market leader Samsung has held 20-30 percent of the market since 2012.) Still, the implicit argument is that Apple's software and hardware designs for the iPhone will mostly lead the way for other phone-makers going forward, as they mostly have for the first decade of the iPhone era.

Still, why should Apple want to do this? The idea here is that Apple's primarily a hardware-and-devices company—which distinguishes Apple from Google, Facebook, Amazon, and Twitter, all of which primarily deliver an internet-based service. Of course, Apple's an internet company too (iTunes, Apple TV, iCloud, and so on), but the company's not hooked on the advertising revenue streams that are the primary fuel for Google, Facebook, and Twitter, or on the sales of other, non-digital merchandise (like Amazon). The ad revenue for the internet-service companies creates what Manjoo argues are "misaligned incentives"—when ad-driven businesses' economic interests lie in getting more users clicking on advertisements, he reasons, he's "skeptical" that (for example) Facebook is the going to offer any real solution to the "addiction" problem. Ultimately, Manjoo agrees with the ThinkDifferentlyAboutKids letter—Apple's in the best position to fix iPhone "addiction" because of their design leadership and independence from ad revenue.

Even so, Apple has other incentives to make iPhones addictive—notably, pleasing its other investors. [126] Still, investors may ultimately be persuaded that Apple-led fixes will spearhead improvements, rooted in our devices, of our social-media experience. (See, for example, this column: *Why Investors May Be the Next to Join the Backlash Against Big Tech's Power.*) [127]

It's worth remembering that the idea technology is addictive is itself an addictive idea—not that long ago, it was widely (although not universally) believed that television was addictive. This *New York Times* story from

125   *Apple iPhone market share 2018*, Statista, https://www.statista.com/statistics/216459/global-market-share-of-apple-iphone/.

126   Trevor Hunnicutt, *IPhone addiction may be a virtue, not a vice for investors*, Reuters (Jan. 8, 2018), https://www.reuters.com/article/us-apple-shareholders-addiction-analysis-idUSKBN1EX2G2.

127   Alex Eule, *Investors Rattle Big Techs Cages*, Barrons (Jan. 13, 2018), https://www.barrons.com/articles/investors-rattle-big-techs-cages-1515818819.

1990 advances that argument, [128] although the reporter does quote a psychiatrist who cautions that "the broad definition" of addiction "is still under debate." (Manjoo's "less addictive iPhone" column inoculates itself, you'll recall, by saying iPhone addiction is "not the same.")

Addiction of course is an attractive metaphor, and certainly those of us who like using our electronics to stay connected can see the appeal of the metaphor. And Apple, which historically has been super-aware of the degree to which its products are attractive to minors, may conclude—or already have concluded, as the ThinkDifferentlyAboutKids folks admit—that more parental controls are a fine idea.

But is it possible that smartphones maybe already incorporate a solution for addictiveness? Just the week before Manjoo's column, another *Times* writer, Nellie Bowles asked whether we can make our phones less addictive just by playing with the settings. (The headline? "Is the Answer to Phone Addiction a Worse Phone?") [129] Bowles argues, based on interviews with researchers, that simply setting your phone to use grayscale instead of color inclines users to respond less emotionally and impulsively—in other words, more mindfully—when deciding whether to respond to their phones. Bowles says she's trying the experiment herself: "I've gone gray, and it's great."

At first it seems odd to focus on the device's user interface (parental settings, or color palette) if the real problem of addictiveness is internet content (social media, YouTube and other video, news updates, messages). One can imagine a *Times* columnist in 1962—in the opening years of widespread color TV—responding to Newt Minow's famous "vast wasteland" [130] speech by arguing that TV-set manufacturers should redesign sets so that they're somewhat more inconvenient—no remote controls, say—and less colorful to watch. (So much for NBC's iconic Peacock opening logo.)

In the interests of science, I'm experimenting with some of these solutions myself. For years already I've configured my iDevices not to

---

128   Daniel Goleman, *How Viewers Grow Addicted To Television*, N.Y. Times (Oct. 16, 1990), https://www.nytimes.com/1990/10/16/science/how-viewers-grow-addicted-to-television.html.

129   Nellie Bowles, *Is the Answer to Phone Addiction a Worse Phone?*, N.Y. Times (Jan. 12, 2018), https://www.nytimes.com/2018/01/12/technology/grayscale-phone.html.

130   Newton N. Minow, Chairman, Fed. Commc'ns Comm'n, Address at the National Association of Broadcasters: Television and the Public Interest (May 9, 1961), https://www.americanrhetoric.com/speeches/newtonminow.htm.

bug me with every Facebook and Twitter update or new-email notice. Plus, I was worried about this grayscale thing on my iPhone X—one of the major features of which is a fantastic camera. But it turns out that you can toggle between grayscale and color easily once you've set gray as the default. I kind of like the novelty of all-gray—no addiction-withdrawal syndrome yet, but we'll see how that goes.

**(5) Social media are bad for us because they make us feel bad, alienating us from one another and causing is to be upset much of the time.** Manjoo says he's skeptical whether Facebook is going to fix the addictiveness of its content and interactions with users, thanks to those "misaligned incentives." It should be said of course that Facebook's incentives—to use its free services to create an audience for paying advertisers—at least have the benefit of being straightforward. (Apple's not dependent on ads, but they still want new products to be attractive enough for users to want to upgrade.) Still, Facebook's Mark Zuckerberg has announced that the company is redesigning Facebook's user experience, [131] (focusing first on its news feed) to emphasize quality time ("time well spent") over more "passive" consumption of the Facebook ads and video that may generate more hits for some advertisers. Zuckerberg maintains that Facebook, even as it has operated over the last decade-plus of general public access, had been good for many and maybe for most users:

> The research shows that when we use social media to connect with people we care about, it can be good for our well-being. We can feel more connected and less lonely, and that correlates with long term measures of happiness and health.

Even so, Zuckerberg writes (translating what Facebook has been hearing from some social-science researchers), "passively reading articles or watching videos—even if they're entertaining or informative—may not be as good." This is a gentler way of characterizing what some researchers have recently been arguing, which is that, for some people at least, using Facebook causes depression. This article for example, relies on sociologist Erving Goffman's conceptions [132] of how we distinguish between our

---

131   Mark Zuckerberg, *One of our big focus areas for 2018 is making sure the time we all spend on Facebook is time well spent,* Facebook (Jan. 11, 2018), https://www. facebook.com/zuck/posts/one-of-our-big-focus-areas-for-2018-is-making-sure-the-time-we-all-spend-on-face/10104413015393571/.

132   *Id.*

public and private selves [133] as we navigate social interactions. Facebook, it's argued, "collapses" our public and private presentations—the result is what social-media researcher danah boyd calls "context collapse." [134] A central idea here is that, because what we publish on Facebook for our circle is also to some high degree public, we are stressed by the need (or inability) to switch between versions of how we present ourselves. In addition context collapse, the highly curated pages we see from other people on Facebook may suggest that their lives are happy in ways that ours are not.

I think both Goffman's and boyd's contributions to our understanding of the sociology of identity (both focus on how we present ourselves in context) are extremely useful, but it's important to think clearly about any links between Facebook (and other social media) and depression. To cut to the chase: there may in fact be strong correlations between social-media use and depression, at least for some people. But it's unclear whether social media actually cause depression; it seems just as likely that causation may go in the other direction. Consider that depression has also been associated with internet use generally (prior to the rise of social-media platforms), with television watching, and even, if you go back far enough, with what is perceived to be excessive consumption of novels and other fiction. [135] Books, of course, are now regarded as redemptive diversions [136] that may actually cure your depression.

So here's a reasonable alternative hypothesis: when you're depressed you seek diversion from depression—which may be Facebook, Twitter, or something else, like novels or binge-watching quality TV. [137] It may be things that are genuinely good for you (books! Or *The Wire*! [138]) or things

---

133  *Dramaturgy (sociology)*, Wikipedia (last edited Jan. 19, 2019), https:// en.wikipedia.org/wiki/Dramaturgy (sociology).

134  Alice E. Marwick & danah boyd, *I tweet honestly, I tweet passionately: Twitter users, context collapse, and the imagined audience*, 13 New Media & Soc'y 114 (2010).

135  Anna North, *When Novels Were Bad For You*, N.Y. Times (Sept. 14, 2014), https:// op-talk.blogs.nytimes.com/2014/09/14/when-novels-were-bad-for-you/.

136  Jay Rayner et al., *A dose of prose: bibliotherapy*, The Guardian (Nov. 27, 2011), https://www.theguardian.com/theobserver/2011/nov/27/school-of-life-biblio-therapy-books.

137  *Does Binge-Watching Make Us Depressed? Good Question*, NPR.org (Feb. 4, 2015), https://www.npr.org/sections/health-shots/2015/02/04/383527370/does-binge-watching-make-us-depressed-good-question.

138  *The Wire* (HBO 2002–2008).

that are unequivocally bad for you. (Don't try curing your depression with drinking!) Or it may be social media, which at least some users will testify they find energizing and inspiring rather than enervating and dispiriting.

As a longtime skeptic regarding studies of internet usage (a couple of decades ago I helped expose a fraudulent article about "cyberporn" usage [139]), I don't think the research on social media and its potential harmful side-effects is any more conclusive than Facebook's institutional belief that its social-media platforms are beneficial. But I do think Facebook as a dominant, highly profitable social-media platform is under the gun. And, as I've written here and elsewhere, its sheer novelty may be generating a moral panic. [140] So it's no wonder—especially now that the U.S. Congress (as well as European regulators) are paying more attention to social media—that we're seeing so many Facebook announcements recently that are aimed at showing the company's responsiveness to public criticism.

Whether you think anxiety about social-media is merited or otherwise, you may reasonably be cynical about whether a market-dominant for-profit company will refine itself to act more consistently in the public interest—even in the face of public criticism or governmental impulses to regulate. But such a move is not unprecedented. [141] The key question is whether Facebook's course corrections—steering us towards personal interactions over "passive" consumption of things like news reports—really do help us. (For example, if you believe in the filter-bubble hypothesis, [142] it seems possible that Facebook's privileging of personal interactions over news may make filter bubbles worse.) This brings us to Problem Number 6, below.

**(6) Social media are bad for us because they're bad for democracy.**
There are multiple arguments that Facebook and other social media

---

139   J Michel Metz, *Misunderstanding Cyberculture: Martin Rimm and the Cyberporn Study*, J Metz's Blog (Mar. 6, 2015), https://jmetz.com/2015/03/misunderstanding-cyberculture-martin-rimm-and-the-cyberporn-study/.

140   *Free Speech and Our Social Media Moral Panic*, Cato Unbound (Jan. 4, 2018), https://www.cato-unbound.org/2018/01/04/mike-godwin/free-speech-our-social-media-moral-panic.

141   *Kingsbury Commitment*, Wikipedia (last edited July 17, 2017), https://en.wikipedia.org/wiki/Kingsbury˙Commitment.

142   *Filter bubble, supra* note 9.

(Twitter's another frequent target) are bad for democracy. *The Verge* provides a good beginning list here.[143] The article notes that Facebook's own personnel—including its awesomely titled "global politics and government outreach director"—are acknowledging the criticisms by publishing a series of blog postings.[144] The first one is from the leader of Facebook's "civic engagement team," and the others are from outside observers, including Harvard law professor Cass Sunstein[145] (who's been a critic of "filter bubbles" since long before that term was invented—his preferred term is "information cocoons.").

I briefly mentioned Sunstein's work in Part 1. Here in Part 2 I'll note mainly that Sunstein's essay for Facebook begins by listing ways in which social-media platforms are actually good for democracy. In fact, he writes, "they are not merely good; they are terrific." In spite of their goodness, Sunstein writes, they also exacerbate what he's discussed earlier (notably in a 1999 paper[146]) as "group polarization." In short, he argues, the filter bubble makes like-minded people hold their shared opinions more extremely. The result? More extremism generally, unless deliberative forums are properly designed with appropriate "safeguards."

Perhaps unsurprisingly, given that Facebook is hosting his essay, Sunstein credits Facebook with taking steps to provide those such safeguards, which in his view includes Facebook chief Mark Zuckerberg's declaration[147] that the company is working to fight misinformation in its news feed. But I like Sunstein's implicit recognition that political polarization, while bad, may be no worse as a result of social media in particular, or even this century's modern media environment as a whole:

---

143   Casey Newton, *The more Facebook examines itself, the more fault it finds*, The Verge (Jan. 22, 2018), https://www.theverge.com/2018/1/22/16920512/facebook-democracy-effects-social-media.

144   Katie Harbath, *Hard Questions: Social Media and Democracy*, Facebook Newsroom (Jan. 2018), http://newsroom.fb.com/news/2018/01/hard-questions-democracy/.

145   Cass R. Sunstein, *Is Social Media Good or Bad for Democracy?*, Facebook Newsroom (Jan. 2018), http://newsroom.fb.com/news/2018/01/sunstein-democracy/.

146   Cass R. Sunstein, *The Law of Group Polarization*, 10 J. Pol. Philosophy 175 (2002).

147   Mark Zuckerberg, *A lot of you have asked what we're doing about misinformation, so I wanted to give an update*, Facebook (Nov. 18, 2016), https://www.facebook.com/zuck/posts/a-lot-of-you-have-asked-what-were-doing-about-misinformation-so-i-wanted-to-give/10103269806149061/.

By emphasizing the problems posed by knowing falsehoods, polarization, and information cocoons, I do not mean to suggest that things are worse now than they were in 1960, 1860, 1560, 1260, or the year before or after the birth of Jesus Christ. Information cocoons are as old as human history.

(I made that argument, in similar form, in a debate with Farhad Manjoo [148]—not then a *Times* columnist—almost a decade ago.)

Just as important, I think, is Sunstein's admission that that we don't really have unequivocal data showing that social media are a particular problem even in relation to other modern media:

> Nor do I mean to suggest that with respect to polarization, social media are worse than newspapers, television stations, social clubs, sports teams, or neighborhoods. Empirical work continues to try to compare various sources of polarization, and it would be reckless to suggest that social media do the most damage. Countless people try to find diverse topics, and multiple points of view, and they use their Facebook pages and Twitter feeds for exactly that purpose. But still, countless people don't.

Complementing Sunstein's essay is a piece by Facebook's Samidh Chakrabarti, who underscores the company's new initiative to make News Feed contributions more transparent (so you can see who's funding a political ad or seemingly authentic "news story"). Chakrabarti also expresses the company's hope that its "Trust Project for News On Facebook" [149] will help users "sharpen their social media literacy." And Facebook's just announced its plan to use user rankings to rate media sources' credibility. [150]

I'm all for more media literacy, and I love crowd-sourcing, and I support efforts to encourage both. But I share CUNY journalism professor Jeff Jarvis's concern that other components of Facebook's comprehensive

---

148   *Mike Godwin on Historically Fragmented Opinion*, Fora TV (Feb. 1, 2012), https://www.dailymotion.com/video/xgjkeu.

149   Andrew Anker, *Launching New Trust Indicators From the Trust Project for News on Facebook*, Facebook Media (Nov. 16, 2017), https://www.facebook.com/facebook-media/blog/launching-new-trust-indicators-from-the-trust-project-for-news-on-facebook.

150   Deepa Seetharaman, *Facebook to Rank News Sources by Quality to Battle Misinformation*, Wall St. J. (Jan. 19, 2018), https://www.wsj.com/articles/facebook-to-rank-news-sources-by-quality-to-battle-misinformation-1516394184.

response to public criticism may unintentionally undercut support,[151] financial and otherwise, for trustworthy media sources.

Now, I'm aware that some critics are arguing that the data really are solidly showing that social media are undermining democracy. But I'm skeptical whether "fake news" on Facebook or elsewhere in social media changed the outcome of the 2016 election, not least because the Pew Research Center's study a year ago suggests that digital news sources weren't nearly as important[152] as traditional media sources. (Notably, Fox News was hugely influential among Trump voters; there was no counterpart news source for Clinton voters.)

That said, there's no reason to dismiss concerns about social media, which may play an increasing role—as Facebook surely has—as an intermediary of the news. Facebook's Chakrabarti may want to promote "social media literacy," and the company has been forced to acknowledge[153] that "Russian entities" tried to use Facebook as an "information weapon." But Facebook doesn't want in the least to play the rule a social-media-literate citizenry should be playing for itself. Writes Chakrabarti:

> In the public debate over false news, many believe Facebook should use its own judgment to filter out misinformation. We've chosen not to do that because we don't want to be the arbiters of truth, nor do we imagine this is a role the world would want for us.

Of course some critics may disagree. As I've said above, the data are equivocal, but that hasn't made its interpreters equivocal. Take for example a couple of recent articles—one academic and another aimed at popular audience—that cast doubt on whether the radical democratization of internet access is a good thing—or at least, whether it's as good a thing as we hoped for a couple of decades ago. One is UC Irvine professor

---

151 Jeff Jarvis, *Facebooks Changes Whither news? Medium*, Whither news? (Jan. 12, 2018), https://medium.com/whither-news/facebooks-changes-235c9089ae40.

152 Amy Mitchell et al., *Trump, Clinton Voters Divided in Their Main Source for Election News*, Pew Research Center's Journalism Project (Jan. 18, 2017), http://www.journalism.org/2017/01/18/trump-clinton-voters-divided-in-their-main-source-for-election-news/.

153 Samidh Chakrabarti, *Hard Questions: What Effect Does Social Media Have on Democracy?*, Facebook Newsroom (Jan. 2018), http://newsroom.fb.com/news/2018/01/effect-social-media-democracy/.

Richard Hasen's law-review article, [154] which he helpfully distilled to a *Los Angeles Times* op-ed. [155] The other is *Wired*'s February 2018 cover story: *It's the (Democracy-Poisoning) Golden Age of Free Speech.* [156] (The *Wired* article is also authored by an academic, UNC Chapel Hill sociology professor Zeynep Tufekci.)

Both Hasen's and Tufekci's articles underscore that internet access has inverted an assumption that long informed free-speech law—that the ability to reach mass audiences is necessarily going to be expensive and scarce. In the internet era, what we have instead is what UCLA professor Eugene Volokh memorably labelled, in a *Yale Law Journal* law-review article more than 20 years ago, as "cheap speech." [157] Volokh correctly anticipated back then that internet-driven changes in the media landscape would lead some social critics to conclude that the First Amendment's broad protections for speech would need to be revised:

> As the new media arrive, they may likewise cause some popular sentiment for changes in the doctrine. Today, for instance, the First Amendment rules that give broad protection to extremist speakers—Klansmen, Communists, and the like-are relatively low-cost, because these groups are politically rather insignificant. Even without government regulation, they are in large measure silenced by lack of funds and by the disapproval of the media establishment. What will happen when the KKK becomes able to conveniently send its views to hundreds of thousands of supporters throughout the country, or create its own TV show that can be ordered from any infobahn-connected household?

There, in a nutshell, is a prediction of the world we're living in now (except that we, fortunately, failed to adopt the term "infobahn"). Hasen believes "non-governmental actors"—that is, Facebook and Twitter and

154 Richard L. Hasen, *Cheap Speech and What It Has Done (to American Democracy)*, 16 First Amendment L. Rev. 200 (2018), https://papers.ssrn.com/sol3/papers.cfm?abstract˙id=3017598.

155 Richard L. Hasen, *Speech in America is fast, cheap and out of control*, L.A. Times (Aug. 18, 2017), https://www.latimes.com/opinion/op-ed/la-oe-hasen-cheap-speech-democracy-20170818-story.html.

156 Zeynep Tufekci, *It's the (Democracy-Poisoning) Golden Age of Free Speech*, Wired (Jan. 16, 2018), https://www.wired.com/story/free-speech-issue-tech-turmoil-new-censorship/.

157 Eugene Volokh, *Cheap Speech and What It Will Do*, 104 Yale L.J. 1805 (1995).

Google and the like—may be "best suited to counter the problems created by cheap speech." I think that's a bad idea, not least because corporate decision-making may be less accountable than public law and regulation and, as Manjoo puts it, they are "misaligned incentives." Tufekci, I think, has the better approach. "[I]n fairness to Facebook and Google and Twitter," she writes in *Wired*, "while there's a lot they could do better, the public outcry demanding that they fix all these problems is mistaken." Because there are "few solutions to the problems of digital discourse that don't involve huge trade-offs," Tufekci insists that deciding what those solutions may be is necessarily a "deeply political decision"—involving difficult discussions what we ask the government to do . . . or not to do.

She's got that right. She's also right that we haven't had those discussions yet. And as we begin them, we need to remember radically democratic empowerment (all that cheap speech) may be part of the problem, but it's also got to be part of the solution.

# Ways Forward for Platforms of Speech

CHAPTER 11

# Everything That's Wrong with Social Media Companies and Big Tech Platforms

*Part 3*

This article was originally published in *Techdirt* on July 16, 2018, at https://www.techdirt.com/articles/20180715/22144840240/everything-thats-wrong-with-social-media-companies-big-tech-platforms-part-3.shtml.

While I could probably turn itemizing complaints about social-media companies into a perpetual gig somewhere—because there's always going to be new material—I think it's best to list only just a few more for now. After that, we ought to step back and weigh what reforms or other social responses we really need. The first six classes of complaints are detailed in Parts 1 and 2, so we begin here in Part 3 with Complaint Number 7.

**(7) Social media are bad for us because they're so addictive to us that they add up to a kind of deliberate mind control.** As a source of that generalization we can do no better than to begin with Tristan Harris's July 28, 2017 TED talk, [158] titled "How a handful of tech companies control billions of minds every day."

Harris, a former Google employee, left Google in 2015 to start a nonprofit organization called Time Well Spent. [159] That effort has now been renamed the Center for Humane Technology ( http://www. timewellspent.io now resolves to https://humanetech.com). [160] Harris says his new effort—which also has the support of former Mozilla interface designer Aza Raskin [161] and early Facebook funder Roger McNamee [162] —represents a social movement aimed at making us more aware of the ways in which technology, including social media and other internet offerings, as well as our personal devices, [163] are continually designed and redesigned to make them more addictive.

Yes, there's that notion of addictiveness again—we looked in Part 2 [164] at claims that smartphones are addictive and talked about how to address that problem. But regarding the "mind control" variation of this criticism, it's worth examining Harris's specific claims and arguments to see how they compare to other complaints about social media and big tech generally. In his June 2017 TED talk. Harris begins with the observation that social-media notifications on your smart devices, may lead you to have thoughts you otherwise wouldn't think:

---

158   Tristan Harris, Address at the TED Conference: How a handful of tech companies control billions of minds every day (July 28, 2017), https://www.youtube.com/watch?v=C74amJRp730.

159   *Time Well Spent*, Wikipedia (last edited Nov. 17, 2018), https://en.wikipedia.org/wiki/Time·Well·Spent.

160   *Center for Humane Technology*, Center for Humane Tech., http://humanetech.com/.

161   *Aza Raskin*, Wikipedia (last edited Jan. 9, 2019), https://en.wikipedia.org/wiki/Aza·Raskin.

162   *Roger McNamee*, Wikipedia (last edited Feb. 2, 2019), https://en.wikipedia.org/wiki/Roger·McNamee.

163   Paul Harper, *Ex-Google boss says you're ADDICTED to your smartphone and it's time to kick the habit*, The Sun (Nov. 29, 2016), https://www.thesun.co.uk/news/2286877/ex-google-boss-says-youre-addicted-to-your-smartphone-and-its-time-to-kick-the-habit/.

164   Mike Godwin, *Everything That's Wrong With Social Media And Big Internet Companies: Part 2*, Techdirt (Jan. 30, 2018), https://www.techdirt.com/articles/20180128/11001839096/everything-thats-wrong-with-social-media-big-internet-companies-part-2.shtml.

If you see a notification it schedules you to have thoughts that maybe you didn't intend to have. If you swipe over that notification, it schedules you into spending a little bit of time getting sucked into something that maybe you didn't intend to get sucked into.

But, as I've suggested earlier in this series, this feature of continually tweaking content to attract your attention isn't unique to internet content or to our digital devices. This is something every communications company has always done—it's why ratings services for traditional broadcast radio and TV exist. Market research, together with attempts to deploy that research and to persuade or manipulate audiences, has been at the heart of the advertising industry for far longer than the internet has existed, as Vance Packard's 1957 book *The Hidden Persuaders*[165] suggested decades ago.

One major theme of Packard's *The Hidden Persuaders* is that advertisers increasingly relied less on consumer surveys (derisively labeled "nose-counting") but on "motivational research"—often abbreviated by 1950s practitioners as "MR"—to look past what consumers say they want. Instead, the goal is to how they actually behave, and then gear their advertising content to shape or leverage consumers' unconscious desires. Packard's narratives in *The Hidden Persuaders* are driven by revelations of the disturbing and even scandalous agendas of MR entrepreneurs and the advertising companies that hire them. Even so, Packard is careful in his book, in its penultimate chapter, to address what he calls "the question of validity"—that is, the question of whether "hidden persuaders' " strategies and tactics for manipulating consumers and voters are actually scientifically grounded. Quite properly, Packard acknowledges that the claims of the MR companies may have been oversold, or may have been adopted by companies who simply lack any other strategy for figuring out how to reach and engage consumers.

In spite of Packard's scrupulous efforts to make sure that no claims of advertising's superpowers to sway our thinking are accepted uncritically, our culture nevertheless has accepted at least provisionally the idea that advertising (and its political cousin, propaganda), affects human beings at pre-rational levels. It is this acceptance of the idea that content somehow takes us over that Tristan Harris invokes consistently in his

---

165   Packard, *supra.*

writings and presentations about how social media, the Facebook newsfeed, and internet advertising work on us.

Harris prefers to describe how these online phenomena affect us in deterministic ways:

> Now, if this is making you feel a little bit of outrage, notice that that thought just comes over you. Outrage is a really good way also of getting your attention. Because we don't choose outrage—it happens to us.

> The race for attention [is] the race to the bottom of the brainstem.

Nothing Harris says about the Facebook newsfeed would have seemed foreign to a Madison Avenue advertising executive in, say, 1957. (Vance Packard includes commercial advertising as well as political advertising as centerpieces of what he calls "the large-scale efforts being made, often with impressive success, to channel our unthinking habits, our purchasing decisions, and our thought processes by the use of insights gleaned from psychiatry and the social sciences.") Harris describes Facebook and other social media in ways that reflect time-honored criticisms of advertising generally, and mass media generally.

But remember that what Harris says about internet advertising or Facebook notifications or the Facebook news feed is true of all communications. It is the very nature of communications among human beings that they give us thoughts we would not otherwise have. It is the very nature of hearing things or reading things or watching things that we can't unhear them, or unread them, or unwatch them. This is not something uniquely terrible about internet services. Instead it is something inherent in language and art and all communications. (You can find a good working definition of "communications" in Article 19 of the United Nations' *Universal Declaration of Human Rights*, which states that individuals have the right "to seek, receive, or impart information.") That some people study and attempt to perfect the effectiveness of internet offerings—advertising or Facebook content or anything else—is not proof that they're up to no good. (They arguably are exercising their human rights!) Similarly, the fact that writers and editors, including me, try to study how words can be more effective when it comes to sticking in your brain is not an assault on your agency.

It should give us pause that so many complaints about Facebook, about social media generally, about internet information services, and about digital devices actively (if maybe also unconsciously) echo complaints that have been made about any new mass medium (or mass-media product). What's lacking in modern efforts to criticize social media in particular—and especially when it comes to big questions like whether social media are damaging to democracy—is the failure of most critics to be looking at their own hypotheses skeptically, seeking falsification (which philosopher Karl Popper rightly notes is a better test of the robustness of a theory[166]) rather than verification.

As for all the addictive harms that are caused by combining Facebook and Twitter and Instagram and other internet services with smartphones, isn't it worth asking critics whether they've considered turning notifications off for the social-media apps?

**(8) Social media are bad for us because they get their money from advertising, and advertising—especially effective advertising—is inherently bad for us.** Harris's co-conspirator Roger McNamee, whose authority to make pronouncements on what Facebook and other services are doing wrong derives primarily from his having gotten richer from them, is blunter in his assessment of Facebook as a public-health menace:

> Relative to FB, the combination of an advertising model with 2.1 billion personalized Truman Shows on the ubiquitous smartphone is wildly more engaging than any previous platform . . . and the ads have unprecedented effectiveness.[167]

There's a lot to make fun of here—the presumption that 2.1 billion Facebook users are just creating "personalized Truman Shows," for example. Only someone who fancies himself part of an elite that's immune to what Harris calls "persuasion" would presume to draw that conclusion about the hoi polloi. But let me focus instead on the second part—the bit about the ads with "unprecedented effectiveness." Here the idea is, obviously, that advertising may be better for us when it's less effective.

Let's allow for a moment that maybe that claim is true! Even if that's so, advertising has played a central role in Western commerce for at least a couple of centuries, and in world commerce for at least a century, and

---

166   *Karl Popper's Falsification*, BBC Radio 4 (Aug. 5, 2015), https://www.youtube. com/watch?v=wf-sGqBsWv4.

167   Roger McNamee, *Brain Hacking for Dummies*, The Well (Mar. 1, 2018), https:// people.well.com/conf/inkwell.vue/topics/504/Brain-Hacking-for-Dummies-page06.html#post137.

the idea that we need to make advertising less effective is, I think fairly clearly, a criticism of capitalism generally. Now, capitalism may very well deserve that sort of criticism, but it seems like an odd critique coming from someone who's already profited immensely from that capitalism.

And it also seems odd that it's focused particularly on social media when, as we have the helpful example of *The Hidden Persuaders* to remind us, we've been theoretically aware of the manipulations of advertising for all of this century and at least half of the previous one. If you're going to go after commercialism and capitalism and advertising, you need to go big—you can't just say that advertising suddenly became a threat to us because it's more clearly targeted to us based on our actual interests. (Arguably that's a feature rather than a bug.)

In responding to these criticisms, McNamee says "I have no interest in telling people how to live or what products to use." (I think the meat of his and Harris's criticisms suggests otherwise.) He explains his concerns this way:

> My focus is on two things: protecting the innocent (e.g., children) from technology that harms their emotion development and protecting democracy from interference. I do not believe that tech companies should have the right to undermine public health and democracy in the pursuit of profits.

As is so often the case with entrepreneurial moral panics, the issue ultimately devolves to "protecting the innocent"—some of whom surely are children but some other proportion of whom constitute the rest of us. In an earlier part of his exploration of these issues on the venerable online conferencing system The WELL, McNamee makes clear, in fact, that he really is talking about the rest of us (adults as well as children):

> Facebook has 2.1 billion Truman Shows . . . each person lives in a bubble tuned to their emotions . . . and FB pushes emotional buttons as needed. Once it identifies an issue that provokes your emotions, it works to get you into groups of like-minded people. Such filter bubbles intensify pre-existing beliefs, making them more rigid and extreme. In many cases, FB helps people get to a state where they are resistant to ideas that conflict with the pre-existing ones, even if the new ideas are demonstrably true.

These generalizations wouldn't need much editing to fit 20th-century criticisms of TV or advertising or comic books or 19th-century criticisms of dime novels or 17th-century criticisms of the theater. What's left unanswered is the question of why this new mass medium is going to doom us when none of the other ones managed to do it.

**(9) Social media need to be reformed so they aren't trying to make us do anything or get anything out of us.** It's possible we ultimately may reach some consensus on how social media and big internet platforms generally need to be reformed. But it's important to look closely at each reform proposal to make sure we understand what we're asking for and also that we're clear on what the reforms might take away from us. Once Harris's TED talk gets past the let-me-scare-you-about-Facebook phase, it gets better—Harris has a program for reform in mind. Specifically, he calls for what he calls "three radical changes to our society," which I will paraphrase and summarize here.

First, Harris says, "we need to acknowledge that we are persuadable." Here, unfortunately, he elides the distinction between being persuaded (which involves evaluation and crediting of arguments or points of view) and being influenced or manipulated (which may happen at an unconscious level). (In fairness, Vance Packard's *The Hidden Persuaders* is guilty of the same elision.) But this first proposition isn't radical at all—even if we're sticks-in-the-mud, we normally believe we are persuadable. It may be harder to believe that we are unconsciously swayed by how social media interact with us, but I don't think it's exactly a radical leap. We can take it as a given, I think, that internet advertising and Facebook's and Google's algorithms try to influence us in various ways, and that they sometimes succeed. The next question then becomes whether this influence is necessarily pernicious, but Harris finds passes quickly over this question, assuming the answer is yes.

Second, Harris argues, we need new models and accountability systems, guaranteeing accountability and transparency for the ways in which our internet services and digital devices try to influence us. Here there's very little to argue with. Transparency about user-experience design that makes us more self-aware is all to the good. So that doesn't seem like a particularly radical goal either.

It's in Harris's third proposal—"We need a design renaissance"—that you actually do find something radical. As Harris explains it, we need to redesign our interactions with services and devices so that we're never persuaded to do something that we may not initially want to do. He states, baldly, that "the only form of ethical persuasion that exists is when the goals of the persuader are aligned with the goals of the persuadee." This is a fascinating proposition that, so far as I know, is not particularly well-grounded in fact or in the history of rhetoric or in the history of ethics. It seems clear that sometimes it's necessary to persuade people of ideas that they may be predisposed not to believe, and that, in fact, they may be more comfortable not believing.

Given that fact, it follows that If we are worried about whether Facebook's algorithms lead to "filter bubbles," we should call for (or design) a system around the idea of never persuading anyone whose goals aren't already aligned with yours. Arguably, such a social-media platform might be more prone to filter bubbles rather than less so. One doesn't get the sense, reviewing Harris's presentations or other public writings and statements from his allies like Roger McNamee, either that they've compared current internet communications with previous revolutions driven by new mass-communications platforms, or analyzed their theories in light of the centuries of philosophical inquiry regarding human autonomy, agency, and ethics.

Moving past Harris's TED talk, we next must consider McNamee's recent suggestion that Facebook move from an advertising-supported to for-pay model. In a February 21 *Washington Post* op-ed, [168] McNamee wrote the following:

> The indictments brought by special counsel Robert S. Mueller III against 13 individuals and three organizations [169] accused of interfering with the U.S. election offer perhaps the most powerful evidence yet that Facebook and its Instagram subsidiary are harming public health and democracy. The best option for the company—and for democracy—is for Facebook to change its business model from one based on advertising to a subscription service.

In a nutshell, the idea here is that the incentives of advertisers, who want to compete for your attention, will necessarily skew how even the

---

168   McNamee, *supra* note 9.

169   Devlin Barrett et al., *Russian troll farm, 13 suspects indicted in 2016 election interference,* Wash. Post (Feb. 16, 2018), https://www.washingtonpost.com/world/national-security/russian-troll-farm-13-suspects-indicted-for-interference-in-us-election/2018/02/16/2504de5e-1342-11e8-9570-29c9830535e5 story.html.

most well-meaning version of advertising-supported Facebook interacts with you, and not for the better. So the fix, he argues, is for Facebook to get rid of advertising altogether. "Facebook's advertising business model is hugely profitable," he writes, "but the incentives are perverse."

It's hard to escape the conclusion that McNamee believes either (a) advertising is inherently bad, or (b) advertising made more effective by automated internet platforms is particularly bad. Or both. And maybe advertising is, in fact, bad for us. (That's certainly a theme of Vance Packard's *The Hidden Persuaders*, as well as of more recent work such as Tim Wu's book 2016 book *The Attention Merchants*.) But it's hard to escape the conclusion that McNamee, troubled by Brexit and by President Trump's election, wants to kick the economic legs out from under Facebook's (and, incidentally, Google's and Bing's and Yahoo's) economic success. Algorithm-driven serving of ads is bad for you! It creates perverse incentives! And so on.

It's true, of course, that some advertising algorithms have created perverse incentives (so that Candidate Trump's provocative ads were seen as more "engaging" and therefore were sold cheaper—or, alternatively, more expensively[170]—than Candidate Clinton's). I think the criticism of that particular algorithmic approach to pricing advertising is valid. But there are other ways to design algorithmic ad service, and it seems to me that the companies that have been subject to the criticisms are being responsive to them, even in the absence of regulation. This, I think, is the proper way to interpret Mark Zuckerberg's newfound reflection (and maybe contrition) over Facebook's previous approach to its users' experience, and his resolve—honoring without mentioning Tristan Harris's longstanding critique—that "[o]ne of our big focus areas for 2018 is making sure the time we all spend on Facebook is time well spent."[171]

**Some Alternative Suggestions for Reform and/or Investigation**  It's not too difficult, upon reflection, to wonder whether the problem of "information cocoons" or "filter bubbles" is really as terrible as some critics have maintained. If hyper-addictive filter-bubbles have historically unprecedented power to overcome our free will, surely presumably have this effect even on most assertive, independently thinking,

---

170   Jonathan Vanian, *Facebook Says Donald Trump Paid More for Online Ads Than Hillary Clinton*, Fortune (Feb. 27, 2018), http://fortune.com/2018/02/27/donald-trump-hillary-clinton-facebook-ads/.

171   Zuckerberg, *supra* note 17.

strong-minded individuals—like Tristan Harris or Roger McNamee. Even six-sigma-degree individualists might not escape! But the evidence that this is, in fact, the case, is less than overwhelming. What seems more likely (especially in the United States and in the EU) is that people who are dismayed by the outcome of the Brexit referendum [172] or the U.S. election [173] are trying to find a Grand Unifying Theory to explain why things didn't work out they way they'd expected. And social media are new, and they seem to have been used by mischievous actors [174] who want to skew political processes, so it follows that the problem is rooted in technology generally or in social media or in smartphones in particular.

But nothing I write here should be taken as arguing that social media definitely aren't causing or magnifying harms. I can't claim to know for certain. And it may well be the case, in fact, that some large subset of human beings create "filter bubbles" for themselves regardless of what media technologies they're using. That's not a good thing, and it's certainly worth figuring out how to fix that problem if it's happening, but focusing on how that problem as a presumed phenomenon specific to social media perhaps focuses on a symptom of the human condition rather than a disease grounded in technology.

In this context, then, the question is, what's the fix? There are some good suggestions for short-term fixes, such as the platforms' adopting transparency measures regarding political ads. That's an idea worth exploring. Earlier in this series I've written about other ideas as well (e.g., using grayscale on our iPhones). [175]

There are, of course, more general reforms that aren't specific to any particular platform. To start with, we certainly need to address more fundamental problems—meta-platform problems, if you will—of democratic politics, such as teaching critical thinking. We actually do

172   *2016 United Kingdom European Union membership referendum*, Wikipedia (last edited Feb. 7, 2019), https://en.wikipedia.org/wiki/2016˙United˙Kingdom˙Europe an˙Union˙membership˙referendum.

173   Drake Baer, *The Filter Bubble Explains Why Trump Won and You Didnt See It Coming*, The Cut (Nov. 9, 2016), https://www.thecut.com/2016/11/how-facebook-and-the-filter-bubble-pushed-trump-to-victory.html.

174   *Russian interference in the 2016 United States elections*, Wikipedia (last edited Feb. 7, 2019), https://en.wikipedia.org/wiki/Russian˙interference˙in˙the˙2016˙United ˙States˙elections.

175   Alex Hern, *Will turning your phone to greyscale really do wonders for your attention?*, The Guardian (June 20, 2017), https://www.theguardian.com/technology/2017/jun/20/turning-smartphone-greyscale-attention-distraction-colour.

know how to teach critical thinking—thanks to the ancient Greeks we've got a few thousand years of work done already on that project—but we've lacked the social will to teach it universally. It seems to me that this is the only way by which a cranky individualist minority that's not easily manipulated by social media, or by traditional media, can become the majority. Approaching all media (including radio, TV, newspapers, and other traditional media—not just internet media, or social media) with appropriate skepticism has to be part of any reform policy that will lead to lasting results.

It's easy, however, to believe that education—even the rigorous kind of education that includes both traditional critical-thinking skills and awareness of the techniques that may be used in swaying our opinions—will not be enough. One may reasonably believe that education can never be enough, or that, even when education is sufficient to change behavior (consider the education campaigns that reduced smoking or led to increased use of seatbelts), education all by itself simply takes too long. So, in addition to education reforms, there probably are more specific reforms—or at least a consensus as to best practices—that Facebook, other platforms, advertisers, government, and citizens ought to consider. (It seems likely that, to the extent private companies don't strongly embrace public-spirited best-practices reforms, governments will be willing to impose such reforms in the absence of self-policing.)

One of the major issues that deserve more study is the control and aggregation of user information by social-media platforms and search services. It's indisputable that online platforms have potentiated a major advance in market research—it's trivially easy nowadays for the platforms to aggregate data as to which ads are effective (e.g., by inspiring users to click through to the advertisers' websites). Surely we should be able to opt out, right?

But there's an unsettled public-policy question about what opting out of Facebook means or could mean. In his testimony earlier this year at Senate and House hearings on Facebook, Mark Zuckerberg has consistently stressed that individual users do have some high degree of control over the data (pictures, words, videos, and so on) that they've contributed to Facebook, and that users can choose to remove the data they've contributed. Recent updates in Facebook's privacy policy[176] seem to underscore users' rights in this regard.

---

176   Laura Hautala, *Facebook's new data policy: Answers to your privacy questions,*
       Cnet (Apr. 21, 2018), https://www.cnet.com/news/facebook-data-policy-answers-

It seems clear that Facebook is committing itself at least to what I call Level 1 Privacy: you can erase your contributions from Facebook altogether and "disappear," at least when it comes to information you have personally contributed to the platform. But does it also mean that even other people who've shared my stuff no longer can share it (in effect, allowing me to depart and punch holes in other people's sharing of my stuff when I depart)?

If Level 1 Privacy relates to the information (text, pictures, video, etc., that I've posted), that's not the end of the inquiry. There's also what I have called Level 2 Privacy, centering on what Facebook knows about me, or can infer from my having been on the service, even after I've gone. Facebook has had a proprietary interest in drawing inferences from how we interact with their service and using that to inform what content (including but not limited to ads) that Facebook serves to us. That's Facebook's data, not mine, because FB generated it, not me. If I leave Facebook, surely Facebook retains some data about me based on my interactions on the platform. (We also know, in the aftermath of Zuckerberg's testimony before Congress, that Facebook manages to collect data about people who themselves are not users of the service.)

And then there's Level 3 Privacy, which is the question of what Facebook can and should do with this inferential data that it has generated. Should Facebook share it with third parties? What about sharing it with governments? If I depart and leave a resulting hole in Facebook content, are there still ways to connect the dots so that not just Facebook itself, but also third-party actors, including governments, can draw reliable inferences about the now-absent me? In the United States, there arguably may be Fourth Amendment issues involved, as I've pointed out in a different context elsewhere.[177] We may reasonably conclude that there should be limits on how such data can be used and on what inferences can be drawn. This is a public-policy discussion that needs to happen sooner rather than later.

Apart from privacy and personal-data concerns, we ought to consider what we really think about targeted advertising. If the criticism of targeted advertising, "motivational research," and the like historically has been that the ads are pushing us, then the criticism of internet advertising seems to be that internet-based ads are pulling us or even seducing us,

---

to-your-privacy-questions-cambridge-analytica/.

177   Godwin, *supra* note 15.

based on what can be inferred about our inclinations and preferences. Here I think the immediate task has to be to assess whether the claims made by marketers and advertisers regarding the manipulative effects ads have on us are scientifically rigorous and testable. If the claims stand up to testing, then we have some hard public-policy questions we need to ask about whether and how advertising should be regulated. But if they aren't—if, in fact, our individual intuitions that we retain freedom and autonomy even in the face of internet advertising and all the data that can be gathered about us—then we need to assert that that freedom and autonomy and acknowledge that, just maybe, there's nothing categorically oppressive about being invited to engage in commercial transactions or urged to vote for a particular candidate.

Both the privacy questions and the advertising questions are big, complex questions that don't easily devolve to traditional privacy talk. If in fact we need to tackle these questions pro-actively, I think we must begin by defining what the problems are in ways that all of us (or at least most of us) agree on. Singling out Facebook is the kind of single-root-cause theory of what's wrong with our culture today may appeal to us as human beings—we all like straightforward storylines—but that doesn't mean it's correct. Other internet services harvest our data too. And non-internet companies have done so (albeit in more primitive ways) for generations. It is difficult to say they never should do so, and it's difficult to frame the contours of what best practices should be.

But if we're going to grapple with the question of regulating social-media platforms and other internet services, thinking seriously about what best practices should be, generally speaking, is the task that lies before us now. Offloading the public-policy questions to the platforms themselves—by calling on Facebook or Twitter or Google to censor antisocial content, for example—is the wrong approach, because it dodges the big questions that we need to answer. Plus, it would likely entrench today's well-moneyed internet incumbents.

Nobody elected Mark Zuckerberg or Jack Dorsey (or Tim Cook or Sundar Pichai) to do that for us. The theory of democracy is that we decide the public-policy questions ourselves, or we elect policymakers to do that for us. But that means we each have to do the heavy lifting of figuring out what kinds of reforms we think we want, and what kind of commitments we're willing to make to get the policies right.

CHAPTER 12

# Are Facebook's Ads Controlling Us? A New Version of an Old Question

This article was originally published in *Lawfare* on May 16, 2018, at https://www.lawfareblog.com/are-facebooks-ads-controlling-us-new-version-old-question.

In the heat of today's debate about the ethics—and possibly anti-democratic effects—of targeted advertising on Facebook and on other internet platforms, it's easy to forget that this debate about advertising is an old one. Do commercial or political advertisers aim to push our psychological buttons in ways we're unaware of? Does advertising really have the power to compel us to buy products or to choose candidates?

In their modern manifestations, these questions hinge on the power of big data, operating together with the presumed accuracy with which our individual tastes and preferences can be tracked and profiled by services like Facebook. But when these same questions were raised in the middle of the last century, they centered on so-called "motivational research" and the so-called social scientists who purported to know more about our tastes and preferences that we might know ourselves.

The mid-20th-century debate about the ethics and aims of advertising accelerated after the publication of Vance Packard's seminal 1957 bestseller, *The Hidden Persuaders*. Packard's narratives are driven by revelations of the disturbing and even scandalous agendas of motivational-research entrepreneurs and the advertising companies that hired them. As Packard writes in his introduction:

> This book is an attempt to explore a strange and rather exotic new area of American life. It is about the large-scale efforts being made, often with impressive success, to channel our unthinking habits, our purchasing decisions, and our thought processes by the use of insights gleaned from psychiatry and the social sciences. Typically these efforts take place beneath our level of awareness; so that the appeals which move us are often, in a sense, "hidden." The result is that many of us are being influenced and manipulated, far more than we realize, in the patterns of our everyday lives.

> Some of the manipulating being attempted is simply amusing. Some of it is disquieting, particularly when viewed as a portent of what may be ahead on a more intensive and effective scale for us all. Cooperative scientists have come along providentially to furnish some awesome tools.

Packard's book sparked a version of the debate about the ethics and morality of advertising that we are now having today The emerging story about Russia's use of Facebook to spread doubt and discord during the 2016 election raises the larger question of whether advertising itself—and especially the targeted, data-driven and data-gathering advertising that subsidizes journalism's internet-based outlets as well as the most successful social-media platforms—is more of a benefit or more of a blight.

Facebook in particular has been criticized as a platform that has empowered advertisers to target in ways that affect us unconsciously, or in ways we can't prevent. Some of Facebook's more prominent critics—notably Tristan Harris and Roger McNamee of the recently-formed Center for Humane Technology—argue that algorithmically shaped online ads, tweaked to our individual tastes and prejudices, overcome our independence and free will in ways that undermine democracy. They've urged that free-to-the-user social-media platforms abandon advertising altogether, switching to a paid-subscription model.

But it's hard to see how the criticisms of advertising on social-media platforms don't apply at least as much to advertising that subsidizes the traditional press, which increasingly relies on both the internet as a conduit and on internet advertising to reach its audiences. (Of course, today's major newspapers, which reach an increasing number of subscribers in their online editions, also take advantage of the data-gathering, audience-shaping technologies deployed by advertisers on the internet—for example, using platforms like Facebook to push out their stories to new readers.) Let's say the *New York Times* or the *Wall Street Journal* cut out advertising altogether. This might reduce the risk that either paper is biased in favor of advertisers' interests, and it would erase the possibility that their ads are manipulating us, but it would also increase the direct cost to readers, maybe by twice as much, or maybe much more. Yet nobody has been seriously suggesting that our major newspapers quit carrying ads.

McNamee, an early investor in Facebook, has recently become highly critical of what he sees as the platform's role in facilitating the election of Donald Trump through enabling Russia's meddling in the 2016 election. But even before that election, McNamee has explained, he was concerned that Facebook shaped the United Kingdom's surprising 2016 vote for Brexit:

> I'm no expert on British politics, but it seemed likely that Facebook might have had a big impact on the vote because one side's message was perfect for the algorithms and the other's wasn't. The "Leave" campaign made an absurd promise—there would be savings from leaving the European Union that would fund a big improvement in the National Health System—while also exploiting xenophobia by casting Brexit as the best way to protect English culture and jobs from immigrants. It was too-good-to-be-true nonsense mixed with fearmongering.

> Meanwhile, the Remain campaign was making an appeal to reason. Leave's crude, emotional message would have been turbocharged by sharing far more than Remain's. . . . [T]he price of Facebook (and Google) ads is determined by auction, and the cost of targeting more upscale consumers gets bid up higher by actual businesses trying to sell them things. As a consequence, Facebook was a much cheaper and more effective platform for Leave in terms of cost per user reached. And filter bubbles would ensure that people on the Leave side would rarely have their questionable

beliefs challenged. Facebook's model may have had the power to reshape an entire continent.[178]

When news reports emerged showing that the Russian Federation had sponsored efforts to interfere in the U.S. election, including efforts using Facebook as a platform, McNamee says, he "formed a simple hypothesis: the Russians likely orchestrated some of the manipulation on Facebook that I had observed back in 2016."[179] He has made clear that he thinks Russian interventions led to the unexpected outcomes in the U.K. and in the United States. Partnering with Harris, McNamee has decried Facebook[180] (and by implication other platforms) for "brain hacking" that overcomes voters' judgment by seducing them into self-imprisonment in "filter bubbles."

As Packard's book reminds us, this concern about advertisers' (and propagandists') potential to overcome the free will, rationality, and independence of the public is not new. But what makes "The Hidden Persuaders" even more useful in the current moment is that Packard is careful to address what he calls "the question of validity"—that is, the question of whether "hidden persuaders' " strategies and tactics for manipulating consumers and voters are actually scientifically grounded. He acknowledges that the claims of the motivational-research companies may have been oversold or may have been adopted by companies who simply lack any other strategy for figuring out how to reach and engage consumers.

Has the advent of the internet and its algorithms that both measure what engages us and suggest what will please us changed "hidden persuasion" into an actual science? McNamee and Harris think so,[181] especially thanks to our current dependence on handheld phones:

> Smartphones changed the advertising game completely. It took
> only a few years for billions of people to have an all-purpose con-

---

178    *How to fix Facebook before it fixes us*, Wash. Monthly (Jan. 7, 2018), https://washingtonmonthly.com/magazine/january-february-march-2018/how-to-fix-facebook-before-it-fixes-us/.

179    *Id.*

180    Asher Schechter, *Roger McNamee: "I Think You Can Make a Legitimate Case that Facebook Has Become Parasitic"*, ProMarket (Mar. 23, 2018), https://promarket.org/roger-mcnamee-think-can-make-legitimate-case-facebook-become-parasitic/.

181    *How to fix Facebook before it fixes us, supra* note 1.

tent delivery system easily accessible sixteen hours or more a day. This turned media into a battle to hold users' attention as long as possible. And it left Facebook and Google with a prohibitive advantage over traditional media. . . . [Their algorithms] appear value neutral, but the platforms' algorithms are actually designed with a specific value in mind: maximum share of attention, which optimizes profits. They do this by sucking up and analyzing your data, using it to predict what will cause you to react most strongly, and then giving you more of that.

But despite what McNamee and Harris argue, there's little independent research[182] that supports their case against "filter bubbles." And there is also plenty of research[183] that calls those fears into question. Likewise, Tim Wu's 2016 book *The Attention Merchants*—which may be regarded as a kind of 21st-century evolution of *The Hidden Persuaders*—carefully dodges the question of scientific validity with the qualitative argument that our attention as human beings is necessarily finite, so that anything that successfully demands our attention does so in a zero-sum game that necessarily eclipses something else that we might have attended to.

Even so, Wu acknowledges early on that human beings are extraordinarily gifted when it comes to screening out things we have no interested in:

The neuroscience of attention, despite having greatly advanced over the past few decades, remains too primitive to explain comprehensively the large-scale harvesting of attention. . . . But there is one thing scientists have grasped that is absolutely essential to understand about the human brain before we go any further: our incredible, magnificent power to ignore.

It's true that to some extent today's internet platforms signify a change: They create more opportunities to tailor ads (and other services) to our interests, not least because the computation power and the ability to collect data has increased rapidly. But it's hardly a settled scientific fact that the new platforms have somehow triumphed over our "magnificent power to ignore." And I don't think we can argue the privacy issues raised

---

182   Dutton, *supra* note 11.

183   Frederik J. Zuiderveen Borgesius et al., *Should we worry about filter bubbles?*, 5 Internet Pol'y Rev. 1 (2016), https://policyreview.info/articles/analysis/should-we-worry-about-filter-bubbles.

by this advertising model as if nobody ever before had the ability to exploit the data we generate with our buying habits and public behaviors before now. What Facebook has actually done, albeit unintentionally, is make it more obvious what things can be known about us. Properly, we should view this development less as a threat than as an opportunity to think more rigorously about the bargains we strike with companies like Facebook as individuals, and the bargains we collectively strike with such companies as a society.

To take one obvious example: Consider the #deletefacebook movement. (And for the sake of this part of the discussion, let's use "Facebook" as a proxy for any social-media company or internet-search giant that may be collecting data about us.) We don't yet have data about how many people are actually following through with their declared interest in opting out of Facebook, but we do know—ironically, thanks to a virtual-private-network-based harvesting of search queries!—that interest in this topic has grown in recent months. [184]

But there's actually an unsettled public-policy question about what opting out of Facebook means or could mean. In his recent testimony before Congress, Facebook CEO Mark Zuckerberg consistently stressed that individual users do have some high degree of control over the data (pictures, words, videos, and so on) that they've contributed to Facebook, and that users can choose to remove the data they've contributed.

Think of this as Level 1 privacy: You can erase your contributions from Facebook altogether and "disappear," at least as an affirmative presence on the platform. But it's worth seeking further clarification as to what such opting out (or opting in and then withdrawing) may mean. Certainly it should mean I can pull down my own content (the pictures and words I posted, for example) and forbid others to use it. It may also reasonably mean that even other people who've shared my stuff no longer can share it (in effect, allowing me to depart and punch holes in other people's sharing of content stuff when I depart). All this is Level 1.

Level 2 is what Facebook knows about me, or can infer from my having been on the service, even after I've gone. Facebook has had a proprietary interest in drawing inferences from how we interact with their service and using that to inform what content (including but not limited to ads) that Facebook serves to us. That's Facebook's data (the

---

184   Jeff Lagerquist, *Delete Facebook movement is strong in Canada, new research shows*, CTVNews (Apr. 20, 2018), https://www.ctvnews.ca/sci-tech/delete-face-book-movement-is-strong-in-canada-new-research-shows-1.3894830.

inferences, that is), because Facebook generated it. (I certainly didn't, and Facebook may in some sense know things about me that I don't myself know.) If I leave Facebook, surely Facebook retains some data about me based on my interactions on the platform. We also know, as a result of Zuckerberg's testimony before Congress, that Facebook manages to collect data about people who themselves are not users of the service.

And then there's Level 3, which is the question of what Facebook can and should do with this inferential data that it has generated. Should it share it with third parties? Should it share it with governments? It seems reasonable to guess that if I depart and leave a Mike Godwin-sized hole in Facebook content, there are still ways to connect the dots so that not just Facebook itself, but also third-party actors, including governments, can draw reliable inferences about the now-absent me. We may reasonably conclude that there should be limits on how such data can be used and on what inferences can be drawn. This is a public-policy discussion that needs to happen sooner rather than later.

Apart from privacy and personal-data concerns, we ought to consider what we really think about targeted advertising. Historically, criticisms of advertising have been similar to criticisms of propaganda—in sum, that advertising may somehow manipulate us into wanting things we shouldn't want and feeling things we shouldn't feel. (This is certainly what we can glean from critics like Packard and Wu.) But the arguments arising from tailored internet-service advertising seem fundamentally different—here the issue isn't so much that we're being influenced to want things we shouldn't want as it is that we're being offered ads that, more and more, are based on larger amounts of data that reflect our actual conscious or unconscious preferences. If the criticism of targeted advertising, "motivational research," and the like historically has been that the ads are pushing us to desire what we otherwise wouldn't have, then the criticism of internet advertising seems to be that internet-based ads are pulling us or even seducing us toward what we already desire, based on what can be inferred about our inclinations and preferences.

As a first step, we should assess whether the claims made by marketers and advertisers regarding the effects ads have on us are scientifically rigorous and testable. (As Packard noted, it's not unheard of for advertising agencies to oversell the effectiveness of the marketing and advertising strategies.) If the claims stand up to testing, then we have some hard public-policy questions we need to ask about whether and how advertising should be regulated.

But if the claims of the new "hidden persuaders" don't stand up to scrutiny, then we should consider that there might be nothing categorically oppressive about being invited to engage in commercial transactions or to embrace a particular political point of view. That's a simpler answer—maybe too simple—but it lines up well with what we have traditionally assumed in democratic societies to be true about freedom of speech and public debate and persuasion in general. In democracies we don't try to control citizens' thoughts, but we do try to persuade citizens, and also to allow ourselves as citizens to be persuaded. So the question that arises with regard to advertising—both consumer advertising and politically driven advertising—is whether we're being subjected to attempts at persuasion or instead to overwhelming tactics of control.

The questions raised about both privacy and advertising are big, complex issues that don't easily devolve to pro- or anti-privacy rhetoric (or pro- or anti-social-media rhetoric). If in fact we need to tackle these questions proactively, we must begin by defining what the problems are in ways that all of us (or at least most of us) agree on. It may be tempting to focus on Facebook, but other internet services harvest our data too. And non-internet companies have done so (albeit in more primitive ways) for generations. It is difficult to say these services never should do so, and it's difficult to frame the contours of what best practices should be.

That said, if we're going to grapple with the question of regulating social-media platforms and other internet services, we need to dig in and think seriously about what best practices should be. Efforts to offload these important public policy questions to the platforms themselves—for example, by calling on Facebook or Twitter or Google to apply their own judgment to censor what they've internally judged to be antisocial content—is a dereliction of Americans' civic duty to craft public policy publicly. If we believe democracy is something worth preserving—and if we have faith in our ability as individuals to resist the pull of advertising and to think skeptically about it—then even if new technologies truly threaten or undermine democracy, we ought nonetheless to use the tools of democratic engagement to save it.

CHAPTER 13

# Is Social Media Broken?

## Part 1: What Do You Do with a Problem like Social Media?

This article was originally published in *Cato Unbound* on December 11, 2017, at https://www.cato-unbound.org/2017/12/11/mike-godwin/what-do-you-do-problem-social-media. The article is a response to Will Rinehart's essay *Fake News and Our Real Problems*, [185] as part of a colloquy titled *Is Social Media Broken?*[186]

The larger theme of this colloquy is whether "social media" are "broken." Will Rinehart's essay hones in on a particular version of that question, which is whether "fake news" is in some sense responsible for course and outcome of the 2016 election. In doing this, he cuts down the "broken-ness" question into something more bite-sized, and hooray for that, because doing so gives us fulcrum we can use for leverage into larger issues.

Will makes many observations that I think are essentially correct, but draws a number of inferences from those observations that I think

---

185   *Fake News and Our Real Problems*, Cato Unbound (Dec. 5, 2017), https://www.cato-unbound.org/2017/12/05/will-rinehart/fake-news-our-real-problems.

186   *Is Social Media Broken?*, Cato Unbound (Dec. 5, 2017), https://www.cato-unbound.org/issues/december-2017/social-media-broken.

may be incorrect or correct but too narrowly gauged. But let's focus at the outset on some things I think he's gotten right.

Will correctly notes that commentators and politicians across the American political spectrum have decried the use of social media platforms to spread disinformation, and that this has led some of these critics to "chide these platforms." He's appropriately skeptical about whether it makes sense to focus on the social media platforms when (he believes) the real focus ought to be on "institutions of governing." (I agree that examining and perhaps reforming these institutions is a necessary condition for American progress, although maybe not a sufficient one.) Will then looks back into the history of how we talk about democracy in the United States. Although I share philosopher Karl Popper's view of the poverty of historicism, [187] I nonetheless think that Rinehart's grounding of modern concerns in historical perspective is generally the right initial approach.

Will's essay veers off into a less useful direction, I think, when he settles on somewhat binary distinction between (a) "modern conceptions" of democracy that stress an informed citizenry and (b) an earlier period of U.S. politics in which "individuals weren't expected to make rational choices when voting." That earlier period, he says, didn't much require that voters know the issues—they just had to pick the candidate or party they preferred. But, per Will's narrative, populist initiatives such as civil-service reform and the secret ballot, together with the rise of national newspapers, weakened party politics by reducing the incentives for party loyalty. With secret ballots, you don't risk riling your neighbors when you vote for Party X in a Party Y district—perhaps because you have been persuaded by a Party-X-leaning national newspaper. But you also don't vote for Party X because it might increase your odds of getting a job as a postmaster or an appointment as a justice of the peace. [188] Thanks to the reforms beginning in the late 19th century, voters and party stalwarts got fewer sticks and also fewer carrots. [189] (Or so it was believed—peer pressure and patronage are slippery beasts that evolve quickly.)

Will correctly notes that our "modern conceptions" of democracy in the United States have as one premise that "the informed citizen" as

---

187    Karl Popper, The Poverty of Historicism (1957).

188    Marbury v. Madison, 5 U.S. (1 Cranch) 137 (1803).

189    *Carrot and stick*, Wikipedia (last edited Feb. 5, 2019), https://en.wikipedia.org/wiki/Carrot˙and˙stick.

a "pillar" supporting what we think makes the American Republic work. And I think he's also right to say that when an election (or an entire election cycle) departs from what's expected—our expectations may be based on polling data and on media accounts—the temptation for our political observers is to seize upon an easy culprit to blame. Because social media are new, still growing, and still transforming our public life, it's easier to target them as the problem, even though Will rightly observes that the available data don't seem to support the trendy idea that Facebook or Twitter or Google are centrally responsible for electoral dysfunction. Americans, like most other world cultures, tend to view new developments in mass media first with fascination and then with alarm lending itself to a moral panic.[190] We saw such a moral panic about porn on the capital-I Internet[191] a couple of decades ago, about television a couple of decades before that,[192] and about consumer-research-based advertising a couple of decades before that.[193] (And don't get me started on video games[194] and comic books.[195])

So, when it comes to Will's underlying thesis—that we should focus more on democratic institutions than on the purported problem of "fake news," he's got both logic and facts on his side. He's right to underscore Jonathan Rauch's comprehensive argument[196] that populist political reforms have been destabilizing. But I wish Will would give more credit to the possibility that social media can actually be a substantive force for good.

In my own international work, I've seen democratic movements in many other countries using Facebook to publicize injustice and mobilize political action. David Kirkpatrick's book *The Facebook Effect* kicks off

---

190  *Moral panic, supra* note 4.

191  Philip Elmer-DeWitt, *Marty Rimm published a controversial study of online porn, and then he disappeared,* Fortune (July 1, 2015), http://fortune.com/2015/07/01/cyberporn-time-marty-rimm/.

192  Jerry Mander, Four Arguments for the Elimination of Television (1978).

193  Packard, *supra* note 8.

194  *Video game controversies,* Wikipedia (last edited Jan. 25, 2019), https://en.wikipedia.org/wiki/Video game controversies.

195  Fredric Wertham, Seduction of the Innocent (1954).

196  Jonathan Rauch, *How American Politics Went Insane,* The Atlantic (June 20, 2016), https://www.theatlantic.com/magazine/archive/2016/07/how-american-politics-went-insane/485570/.

with an account of how a single Facebook user in Colombia leveraged the social-media platform to mobilize public opposition to the FARC guerilla movement. These uses of social media (yes, Instagram and Twitter play their roles here as well) ought to be the centerpieces of any argument that social media aren't, in fact, "broken."

But Will's not-so-ringing defense against the charge that social media are "broken" or that they facilitate the spread of "fake news" is this:

> What people do online is engage in the pointless babble that is so often derided. They go online to express sociability and maintain bonds, not debate politics. Snapchat isn't built on political rants, it is built on videos and pictures of family, pets, and the sweet banality of daily life. Much more social media is like this than we tend to imagine.

So we shouldn't worry about social media because they're more or less inconsequential "babble"? Nice try, but as the Supreme Court has shown us, it's a lot easier to justify censorship of any exercise of freedom of expression if you can show that it lacks "serious literary, artistic, political, or scientific value." [197] Even if only a few social-media users leverage their platforms for political expression, I'd take that to mean that the platforms definitely do have "serious" political value.

But I'd make the argument that even what Will dismisses as "pointless babble" does in fact have a point. Expressing sociability and maintaining bonds is, in my view, as central to making the American republic work as debating politics is. It's also central to our understanding of the First Amendment, which we generally understand to protect any kind of expressive communication—including what Thomas Emerson characterized in 1963 as the First Amendment's support of "individual self-fulfillment" [198]—not just political debates. What's more, it's clear that the social media we may first explore for fun or "the sweet banality of everyday life" are tools that, thanks to our hands-on experience, we can later leverage in political processes. Even if, as Will states, 2016 wasn't "the election of social media," there's no particular reason think 2020 won't be. And it's likely than that Jonathan Rauch's suggested reforms—

---

197   Miller v. California, 413 U.S. 15 (1973).

198   Thomas I. Emerson, *Toward a General Theory of the First Amendment*, 72 Yale L.J. 877 (1963), https://digitalcommons.law.yale.edu/fss papers/2796.

aimed at strengthening political-party organizations—won't be in place before then. Rauch writes:

> The biggest obstacle [to strengthening political parties] is the general public's reflexive, unreasoning hostility to politicians and the process of politics. Neurotic hatred of the political class is the country's last universally acceptable form of bigotry. Because that problem is mental, not mechanical, it really is hard to remedy.[199]

If hatred of politics and politicians is a mental problem, then maybe we need to address it as a nation through talk therapy: the group therapy[200] of social media. No one can seriously dispute that, whatever else these platforms are used for, individuals use them a lot nowadays to express concerns about our political process and to chart a path forward.

Will asserts that "[f]rom the very founding of the United States until the late 1890s, individuals weren't expected to make rational choices when voting" and that, post-populist-reforms, we're still in need of what Michael Schudsen called "a language of public life that reconciles democracy and expertise."[201] But that's not my takeaway even from the most anti-majoritarian passages of The Federalist, which, in number 22, underscores that "[t]he fabric of American empire ought to rest on the solid basis of THE CONSENT OF THE PEOPLE." (No one discouraged Publius from using all-caps.) Presumptively in our republic, the people have the expertise to pick leaders with governmental expertise.

Of course, sometimes the people make bad decisions in voting. Whether you exalt the wisdom of crowds[202] or decry the madness of crowds,[203] the fact is that crowds are at the heart of making our republic work. Sure, sometimes our crowds do goofy things, but sometimes they do the right thing. Free-market theory[204] recognizes that crowds may know more than even the best experts, but economic booms and busts

---

199  Rauch, *supra* note 12.

200  *Group psychotherapy*, Wikipedia (last edited Nov. 10, 2018), https://en.wikipedia. org/wiki/Group˙psychotherapy.

201  Democracy and New Media (Henry Jenkins & David Thorburn eds., 2003).

202  James Surowiecki, The Wisdom of Crowds (2005).

203  Charles Mackay, Memoirs of Extraordinary Popular Delusions (Richard Bentley 1841), https://catalog.hathitrust.org/Record/008681491.

204  *Friedrich Hayek*, Wikipedia (last edited Feb. 6, 2019), https://en.wikipedia.org/ wiki/Friedrich˙Hayek.

show us how all too frequently there's a lag time as our crowds advance up the learning curve. [205] For me, the prospect of our crowd's sharing personal and political knowledge and even wisdom directly with one another—rather than, say, merely through the imperfect signaling of prices—is a central promise of social media. Yes, our social-media platforms are certainly imperfect, but they're also evolving, not least because they do have a stake in listening to our complaints. They're not "broken" any more than a baby who can crawl but can't yet walk is "broken." What they are, instead, is a work in progress. What we need to do when social media manifest social dysfunction is give them—and us—the space in which to grow up.

---

205  *New Keynesian economics,* Wikipedia (last edited Dec. 2, 2018), https:// en.wikipedia.org/wiki/New˙Keynesian˙economics.

CHAPTER 14

# Is Social Media Broken?

## *Part 2: Beyond Free Speech Narrowly Considered*

---

This article was originally published in *Cato Unbound* on December 22, 2017, at https://www.cato-unbound.org/2017/12/22/mike-godwin/beyond-free-speech-narrowly-considered. The article is a response to Will Rinehart's essay *Fake News and Our Real Problems*, [206] as part of a colloquy titled *Is Social Media Broken?* [207]

---

Like John Samples, [208] I find Thomas I. Emerson's [209] exploration of the social value of the First Amendment persuasive, and it has been profoundly influential on my thinking as a civil libertarian. Freedom of speech, as Emerson explains, is valuable for more than just its necessity to the proper function of democracy, and John particularly underscores this point when he says that, in terms of free speech's role in individual self-fulfillment, "social media is an unalloyed good."

---

206    *Fake News and Our Real Problems, supra.*

207    *Is Social Media Broken?, supra.*

208    *Social Media and the First Amendment's Values,* Cato Unbound (Dec. 8, 2017), http://www.cato-unbound.org/2017/12/08/john-samples/social-media-first-amendments-values.

209    Thomas I. Emerson, The System of Freedom of Expression (1970).

Dovetailing nicely with John's channeling of Emerson is Kate Klonick's discussion, [210] which points us to Yale law professor Jack Balkin's great 2004 article [211] about "digital speech and democratic culture." Kate argues that our democratic culture is bigger than just voting—or politics generally, and I'm compelled to agree. Fans of Balkin's 2004 article—and I count myself among them—will likely also enjoy Balkin's more recent articles that address the intersection of the public interest, government power, and the companies that operate the internet's digital platforms. (You can start with Balkin's recent law-review article [212]—summarized helpfully in Balkin's blog post earlier this year [213]—and trace it through its footnotes to Balkin's developing an increasingly systematic appraisal of internet culture and its relationship to our law and values. Taken together, Balkin's articles are must reading for anyone grappling with the impact and implications of today's social media and other internet platforms.)

And I especially like Kate's conclusion:

> To focus a discussion about the internet's role in democracy only on its ability to enable discussions of pure politics or information for actual voting is like arguing that one leg of a stool is the most important. Instead, the real concern for democracy should be not on fake news but instead on preserving free speech online in order to continue to enable a robust and vibrant democratic culture.

All too often, we allow ourselves to yield to the easy temptation to understand freedom of expression in terms of its political, democratic value. I perhaps differ from Will in that I may think freedom of expression, including what he dismisses as "babble," is more central to governance of our democratic republic than he does.

---

210   *Democratic Culture Is More than Mere Voting*, Cato Unbound (Dec. 14, 2017), https://www.cato-unbound.org/2017/12/14/kate-klonick/democratic-culture-more-mere-voting.

211   Jack M. Balkin, *Digital Speech and Democratic Culture: A Theory of Freedom of Expression for the Information Society*, 79 N.Y.U. L. Rev. 1 (2004), https://www.nyulawreview.org/issues/volume-79-number-1/digital-speech-and-democratic-culture/.

212   Balkin, *supra* note 8.

213   Jack Balkin, *The Pluralist Model of Speech Regulation: Free Speech in the Algorithmic Society*, Balkinization (Sept. 18, 2017), https://balkin.blogspot.com/2017/09/the-pluralist-model-of-speech.html.

Furthermore, I'd argue that my more expansive view of the importance of freedom of expression, especially on comparatively new platforms like social media, reflects a more expansive consensus about the value of freedom of speech in the modern era. That is, I think, the thrust of what Balkin discusses in his 2004 article when he criticizes the Alexander Meiklejohn tradition of free-speech-to-promote-democratic-deliberation as "only a partial conception, inadequate to deal with the features of speech that the new digital technologies bring to the foreground of our concern."

This expansive consensus about freedom-of-expression functions that we in the United States associate primarily with our First Amendment are also recognized and supported—not for their mere political value but simply as individual liberties—by other national and international rights instruments around the world, including the International Covenant on Civil and Political Rights. Most modern governments either commit themselves to freedom of expression as individual liberty—including how this liberty is exercised on social media—or else they at least try to give the appearance of doing so. Even the lip service to free speech that most nondemocratic governments offer nowadays is a sign of progress—only a few centuries ago governments' talk of the need to protect individual liberty was the exception rather than the rule.

In my own work as an advocate of online freedom of expression, recognizing that we always need to consider online freedom of expression in terms of its wider individual-liberty importance rather than in terms of its importance to democratic governance, came to me as an epiphany back in 1995. That's when I listened to a fellow speaker at a University of Texas event (the Austin institution is my alma mater) decry how people were exercising their freedom of speech on the newly arrived internet. As I recounted in *Wired* that year, [214] my fellow speaker was ready to dismiss the importance of internet speech that isn't directly concerned with political change:

> If the Internet is such a tool of democracy, [Gary] Chapman wondered, why isn't it being used to organize activist projects? Instead, Chapman complained, net-folks too often choose to exercise their vaunted freedom of speech by focusing on "trivia and sleaze." This is troubling, he said, because the purpose of freedom of speech is to inspire and promote social and political progress—to "stimulate

214   Godwin, *supra* note 8.

collective action." For Chapman, "effective, potent free speech"—the kind that leads to progressive political results in the physical world—is morally superior to the anarchic, selfish free speech of the Net, which is "palpably disengaged" (how does one "palpate" disengagement?) from the crises facing our nation.

So when Will described most use of social-media platforms as "pointless babble"—although allowing that sometime this "banality" is "sweet"—I heard echoes of the same dismissiveness of internet freedom of expression that I believed more than two decades ago might pave the way for a new imposition of censorship. I still worry about that today, especially in light of the current wave of arguments that social media or the companies that currently host these platforms are out of control and socially destructive. [215] My response now, as it was then, is that the social channels of expression we adopt for fun will ultimately turn out to be instruments not only of fundamental individual liberty but also of democratically driven social progress.

To be sure, I understand and sometimes empathize with the impulse to constrain social media—it's new, rapid-response, and sometimes sometimes scarily powerful. (That's why I think Kate's focus on the #metoo movement in this year's social media is spot-on.) I even sympathize a little bit with the impulse to take a "hard break" from social media, as one former Facebook executive urged recently. [216] But my own experience suggests that, rather than take a "hard break," it serves us all better to take a few breaths. The current moral panic about social media [217] isn't the first one our culture has had to process—consider, for example, the worries about cheap paper [218]—and it won't be the last. We owe it to our posterity to treasure and defend the new liberty we've got, not just because it helps us govern ourselves, but because it helps us become ourselves.

---

215    James Vincent, *Former Facebook exec says social media is ripping apart society*, The Verge (Dec. 11, 2017), https://www.theverge.com/2017/12/11/16761016/former-facebook-exec-ripping-apart-society.

216    *Id.*

217    Mike Godwin, *Everything That's Wrong With Social Media And Big Internet Companies: Part 1*, Techdirt (Nov. 29, 2017), https://www.techdirt.com/articles/20171128/23565738694/everything-thats-wrong-with-social-media-big-internet-companies-part-1.shtml.

218    Adler, *supra* note 4.

CHAPTER 15

# Is Social Media Broken?

## Part 3: Free Speech and Our Social Media Moral Panic

This article was originally published in *Cato Unbound* on January 4, 2018, at https://www.cato-unbound.org/2018/01/04/mike-godwin/free-speech-our-social-media-moral-panic. The article is a response to Will Rinehart's essay *Fake News and Our Real Problems*,[219] as part of a colloquy titled *Is Social Media Broken?*[220]

I'm grateful that Will Rinehart has taken pains to respond not only conversationally[221] to our reactions to his initial essay but also with a more essayistic effort to try to frame the role of social media in a larger theory of democracy.[222] I'm going to respond to all of these efforts here, because I think, even taken together, Will's three contributions fall short in addressing both (a) the overarching question of whether social media

219   *Fake News and Our Real Problems, supra.*

220   *Is Social Media Broken?, supra.*

221   *Democracy as an Essentially Contested Concept,* Cato Unbound (Dec. 21, 2017), https://www.cato-unbound.org/2017/12/21/will-rinehart/democracy-essentially-contested-concept.

222   *Technologies of Freedom,* Cato Unbound (Jan. 3, 2018), https://www.cato-unbound.org/2018/01/03/will-rinehart/technologies-freedom.

are "broken" and (b) the equally important question of how we should think about social media in the context of our democratic values.

In thinking through my reactions to Will's three pieces, I'm drawn back to the contributions of my fellow contributors to this colloquy, John Samples [223] and Kate Klonick. [224] John's response essay is framed in terms of Thomas Emerson's helpful taxonomy of the functions of freedom of expression, first spelled out here [225] and later explored in his subsequent books. Kate's response drew upon Nicholas Tampio's articulation of the value of democracy [226] as well as Jack Balkin's 2004 law review article [227] arguing that freedom of expression—a bigger set of interests than just talking about politics—needs to be affirmatively protected, not just by the courts, but also by the legislators, administrative agencies, and technology players who increasingly shape the space in which digital speech takes place.

My own initial response also drew upon Emerson and Balkin, though I've drawn primarily on later works by both scholars, and I urge readers who may be diverted by Klonick's and Samples's discussions of Balkin's 2004 article to consider how Balkin's free-speech thinking has evolved since then, starting here. [228] So I was interested to see how Will would respond to what I think all three of his respondents have in common. Specifically, we all addressed the question of how to root our understanding of social media in First Amendment theory and our theory of democracy generally.

I think Will's lead essay and his responses, taken together, gesture in the direction of a theory of democracy and social media that simultaneously asserts a "thin" assessment of their value while dismissing their real importance. As part of his dismissal of the importance of the democracy/ free-expression/social-media nexus, Will makes a number of rhetorical moves, all of which I take to be aimed at marginalizing the larger perspective

---

223   *Social Media and the First Amendment's Values, supra* note 3.

224   *Democratic Culture Is More than Mere Voting, supra* note 5.

225   Emerson, *supra* note 14.

226   Nicholas Tampio, *Why rule by the people is better than rule by the experts Nicholas Tampio*, Aeon (Oct. 18, 2017), https://aeon.co/essays/why-rule-by-the-people-is-better-than-rule-by-the-experts.

227   Balkin, *supra* note 6.

228   Balkin, *supra* note 8.

on social media that, in different ways, John, Kate, and I tried to import into the discussion question of whether social media are "broken."

I believe that our three initial responses to Will's lead essay share a resistance to the constrictiveness of Will's focus on whether "fake news" is a problem that somehow tells us something about social media. Here's why I think the narrowness of Will's initial approach and the dismissiveness in his follow-up responses leaves me unsatisfied. Basically, if you read a lot of the recent mainstream opinion writing about social media—not just op-eds but also recent books like Jonathan Taplin's and Franklin Foer's—it seems clear that some would-be opinion leaders are trying to gin up a consensus that, yes, social media are "broken"—that there's something going on with regard to social media that needs to be fixed.

Unsurprisingly, the critics who are advancing this argument are unswayed by research that seems to show that "fake news" may not have had an appreciable effect on the outcome of the 2016 elections. The critics argue that in a presidential election as close as the 2016 election was, even small distortions in voter response, possibly attributable to "fake news," may have altered the outcome, and that the research that casts doubt on this hypothesis is ambiguous at best. This argument isn't crazy on its face. I'm skeptical whether "fake news" had such an effect in the last election, but I also think reasonable people can disagree about that, and that reasonable people can reasonably worry whether internet media will help or hurt upcoming elections.

So it seems clear to me that the concern about "fake news" and about other possible negative impacts of social media are going to be with us for a while. We can't just say "social media didn't screw up the 2016 election," dust off our hands, and walk away.

But it's hard for me to escape the impression that this is what Will has been trying to do. Let me explain my reasoning here.

In my view, Will's first essay[229] included a couple of theses. First, he seems to argue that American democracy is rooted less in voter access to accurate information (he dismisses this as part of the "folk theory of democracy") than what might be called (presumably irrational) partisan affiliation:

> From the very founding of the United States until the late 1890s, individuals weren't expected to make rational choices when voting. Not surprisingly, the press was explicitly partisan.

229 *Fake News and Our Real Problems, supra* note 1.

Newfangled reforms like those championed by the Progressive movement, together with the rise of emphasis on journalistic "objectivity," apparently led to the supplanting of this political tribalism with the "folk theory of democracy," which is dismissible because it doesn't give adequate weight to expertise. (Will quotes Michael Schudson here about the "quest for a language of public life that reconciles democracy and expertise.")

A second thesis in Will's first essay was that the available research doesn't support the idea that "2016 was the election of social media" and that, in any case, people mainly use social media for "pointless babble" rather than to inform themselves or to argue politically.

In different ways, John's, Kate's, and my responses tried to offer stronger cases in defense of social media than what Will provided. But it seems to me that Will's initial response and his follow-up essay attempted to dodge those defenses altogether. Instead, Will raised the issue that democracy is "an essentially contested concept." It seems possible that Will was aiming to characterize the extent to which the responses to his first essay disagreed as one that's rooted in different notions of democracy, so that if the three response essays differ with his reasoning, it's because we're using a different, broader idea (or ideal) of democracy than Will uses.

But taking that approach doesn't make the case for dismissing these ideas or ideals. It especially doesn't make the case for dismissing Jack Balkin's 2004 law review article as "the kind of language game with democracy that [W.B. Gallie] lays out." To understand Balkin's article as playing a "language game" at all is to mischaracterize the century of First Amendment scholarship on which Balkin draws, and to which he was responding. Specifically, Balkin's article expressly addresses what might be called the Alexander Meiklejohn approach to the First Amendment,[230] one in which the importance of freedom of speech is, centrally, its importance to democratic government—to making politics and elections work properly in a democracy. Like many other constitutional lawyers (including yours truly) Balkin is critical of Meiklejohn's narrow theory of the First Amendment (that it's primarily about politics).

But even Meiklejohn's comparatively narrow First Amendment theory, which focuses on informing citizens about political choices, is broader than Will's. As I read him, Will thinks the notion that an accurately

---

230   Alexander Meiklejohn, Free speech and its relation to self-government (1948).

informed voting population is valuable is a kind of populist, "folk" myth. Ironically, Balkin's push for understanding freedom of expression more broadly in the digital age is as much a challenge to the free-speech-for-good-politics idea as Will's dismissal of the "folk theory of democracy" is—it's just coming at it from the other direction. This is the same thing that Thomas Emerson's theory, which informs John Samples's response essay,[231] does.

Understanding the importance of free speech broadly, as Balkin's 2004 article does, is something that, in my view, you also see in John's, Kate's, and my initial responses. I think Will recognized, after drafting his first response, that our essays needed a more substantive response than an implicit dismissal, and that this recognition is what has fueled his longer, second essay.[232]

My view is that Will's first response more or less dodged the arguments that freedom of expression, including how it is exercised in social media, has democratic value much bigger than how it affects or doesn't affect elections. His longer essay, his third contribution after his lead essay, and initial response attempt to challenge John's, Kate's, and my responses more squarely. But in doing so, Will fundamentally mischaracterizes both the implicit and express criticisms as representing what he believes are naïve "emancipatory visions" of the internet. Will attributes one "version of the emancipated world" to Ithiel de Sola Pool, but I think Pool's magnum opus[233] is properly read as a clear-eyed assessment of where government policy can either enhance freedom (as it has done with the First Amendment and with common carriage)—or undermine freedom (as it has done in broadcasting) rather than serving as a standalone dream of how wonderfully the internet might emancipate us.

I had to wince at that point when I came across the words "emancipatory visions"; I could see where Will was going next. And, sure enough, Will invokes my friend Howard Rheingold's observation that the early days of internet activism were informed by, inter alia, "granola-eating utopians, the solar-power enthusiasts, serious ecologists and the space-station crowd, immortalists." And then, inevitably, he quotes my friend and

---

231  *Social Media and the First Amendment's Values, supra* note 3.

232  *Democracy as an Essentially Contested Concept, supra* note 3.

233  Ithiel de Sola Pool, Technologies of Freedom: On Free Speech in an Electronic Age (1983).

former colleague John Perry Barlow's "now notorious" Declaration of Independence for Cyberspace.

Here I must share some late-breaking news from the 1990s: the actual cyber-activists of that period (and here I must include myself) did not interpret Barlow's *cri de coeur* as political philosophy. Barlow, best known prior to his co-founding of the Electronic Frontier Foundation as a songwriter for the Grateful Dead, was writing to inspire activism, not to prescribe a new world order, and his goal was to be lyrical and aspirational, not legislative. Barlow wrote and published his "Declaration" in the short days and weeks after Congress passed, and President Clinton signed into law, a telecommunications bill that aimed, in part, to censor the internet. No serious person—and certainly not the Electronic Frontier Foundation and other organizations that successfully challenged the Communications Decency Act provisions of that bill—believed that cyberspace would be "automagically" independent of the terrestrial world and its governments. Barlow's "Declaration" is best understood, as *Wired* described it two decades later,[234] as a "rallying cry." Similarly, nobody thinks "The Star-Spangled Banner" or "America the Beautiful" or "This Land Is Your Land" is a constitution. (And of course the original Declaration of Independence isn't one either.)

I confess that I invoked Barlow's incantatory rhetoric on a single celebratory occasion.[235] But I did so precisely because I believe a declaration of independence by its very nature should not and cannot be interpreted as a prospective theory of governance. (Compare: "All men are created equal.") So when I delivered a public speech on the day we celebrated a unanimous Supreme Court victory for the First Amendment in cyberspace,[236] "[n]ow is the time to think about what kind of First Amendment we will shape for ourselves and for those who come after us."[237] In other words, the hard work of protecting freedom of speech on the internet was still just beginning, and we still had the task before us to figure out how the rule of law would apply there. In

---

234 Andy Greenberg, *Its been 20 years since John Perry Barlow declared cyberspace independence*, Wired (Feb. 8, 2016), https://www.wired.com/2016/02/its-been-20-years-since-this-man-declared-cyberspace-independence/.

235 David Hudson, *Net freedom ring*, Salon.com (July 1, 1998), https://www.salon.com/1998/07/01/books`11/.

236 *Reno*, 521 U.S. 844.

237 Godwin, *supra* note 7.

any case, just as Barlow's rallying cry wasn't political theory, my citing it in a celebratory speech wasn't either.

As a pragmatic matter—as distinct from the "emancipatory vision" Will dismisses—the very reason we mounted the constitutional challenge to that legislation is precisely because we believed that freedom of expression in cyberspace was utterly dependent on what governments in the physical world might do or attempt to do in pursuit of silencing troublesome speech.

Will oddly invokes the Free Press as another exemplar of the "emancipatory bent," quoting a 2008 statement from Free Press's website that I will quote more fully here:

> But whether the Internet remains open, diverse and democratic depends largely on policy decisions. If past is prologue, the prospects aren't good. Over the past 100 years, whenever a "disruptive technology"—such as radio or television broadcasting—sparked democratic participation in media, dominant forces reacted by creating rules to lock it down, stifle public participation and reassert their authority.

It is difficult to understand what point about "emancipatory visions" that Will is trying to make, given that he's quoting Free Press right after quoting Barlow's Declaration of Independence for Cyberspace. Sure, Barlow can be interpreted by (absurdly) literal readers as saying a bunch of factually untrue things—for example "Our identities have no bodies, so, unlike you, we cannot obtain order by physical coercion"—which most adults will understand to be an exercise of Barlow's poetic license.

But what the Free Press says regarding the disruptive media technologies and the legislative and regulatory responses to them is indisputably, factually true. Media scholars of different political persuasions actually agree that this has been a common governmental reaction to new mass-media platforms. My favorite account of the paroxysms of broadcasting regulation—including the thinness of the theoretical justifications of that regulation—was written by one of my law-school professors, Lucas A. Powe. [238] It seems possible that Will wants to rope in Free Press here as part of his dismissal of "emancipatory visions" because Free Press is openly advocating the net neutrality regulations that Will opposes. But the original "emancipatory vision" of Barlow's Declaration

---

238    Lucas A. Powe, Jr., American Broadcasting and the First Amendment (1987).

of Independence was one of denying terrestrial governments' ability to regulate the internet. Regardless of one's opinion of net neutrality, it's quite clear that net-neutrality advocates actually believe terrestrial governments do have jurisdiction and do have power—not, as Barlow lyricizes, that they don't.

In the circumstances, it seems possible that what Will views as "emancipatory politics" is a simply an optimistic vision that Will doesn't agree with. And this brings us precisely to Will's parachuting in the estimable Adam Thierer's insightful 2010 essay[239] about the oscillations between "technological pessimists" and the technophile "pollyannas." I love Thierer's essay not least because he underscores how the techno-pessimist philosopher Neil Postman, citing Plato's Phaedrus in his 1992 book *Technopoly*, was "fancying himself a bit of a modern King Thamus." King Thamus, you may recall, was the king whom Plato depicts as opposing the invention of writing. Of course Neil Postman relied on the invention of writing to compose *Technopoly*.

Thierer in his essay, and in many other writings and appearances since, has called for "pragmatic optimism," which Will characterizes as "a sensible middle ground position." I think so too—and "pragmatic optimism" is pretty much the only approach you can use if you're a civil libertarian who seeks to defend freedom of speech on the internet and elsewhere. You have to be pragmatic in order to recognize clearly where the challenges to internet freedom and privacy come from, and you have to be optimistic just to get up in the morning to address those challenges—in cases, for example, or in legislation or regulation. And although he counsels pragmatism, Thierer makes no secret of which party he belongs to: "On balance, I believe the optimists generally have the better of the argument today."

But even the "sensible" notion of pragmatic optimism—an approach that I think has informed my own work on internet law and policy over the last three decades—is too optimistic for Will's taste. Although, as he writes, "Thierer is right to be optimistic about the possibilities of new technologies," "[internet-based] technologies are still judged by those emancipatory visions formed at the early stages of technology."

---

239    Adam Thierer, *Are You An Internet Optimist or Pessimist? The Great Debate over Technology's Impact on Society*, Tech. Liberation Front (Jan. 31, 2010), https://tech-liberation.com/2010/01/31/are-you-an-internet-optimist-or-pessimist-the-great-debate-over-technology%e2%80%99s-impact-on-society/.

I confess I have at this last sentence many times tried to figure out what it means, or how Will means to be taken to dissent from Thierer's pragmatic optimism or from mine. Plus, if "emancipatory visions" are the dominant paradigm in evaluating the internet, how do we explain the flood of writing this year ranging from Al Franken's last major op-ed as senator [240] to Jonathan Taplin's anti-tech-giant screed [241] and Franklin Foer's blaming the loss of his sweet gig at The New Republic on the internet companies' undermining of "the culture industries"? [242] Indeed, if "emancipatory politics" is somehow today's dominant paradigm, why are we even discussing here whether social media are "broken"? Why isn't our consensus reality simply that the internet and social-media platforms are an unalloyed blessing?

I think the answer to this question has to be that many of us recognize a moral panic occurring in our culture (and in other cultures around the world) about the internet and social media. It's a moral panic that both predates last year's election and is not particularly rooted in that election. I have begun to write about that moral panic here, [243] and Adam Thierer's recent review of Foer's book is titled "Franklin Foer's Tech-Panic Manifesto." [244] So if we're going to talk about whether social media are "broken," we have to do so in express recognition of the moral panic about social media that's happening. We have to ground our arguments in theories that speak positively of what social media have given us, not merely dismissively with the notion that this "pointless babble" has probably not done any great harm.

To his credit, Will tries to break some new ground in terms of a positive defense with what he calls "the capabilities approach," which he characterizes as both an "evaluative framework" that "isn't a series of answers, but a more formalized series of questions." The capabilities approach, he says, is one of evaluating "various aspects of individual wellbeing" and, in that light, "a tool to design and evaluate policies." This

240   Franken, *supra* note 6.

241   Nick Romeo, *New book 'Move Fast and Break Things' takes on Amazon, Face-bok, Google*, Chicagotribune.com (Apr. 19, 2017), https://www.chicagotribune.com/lifestyles/books/sc-move-fast-and-break-things-jonathan-taplin-books-0419-20170418-story.html.

242   Kolbert, *supra* note 3.

243   Godwin, *supra* note 12.

244   Adam Thierer, *Franklin Foer's Tech-Panic Manifesto*, Reason.com (Dec. 23, 2017), https://reason.com/archives/2017/12/23/how-to-write-a-tech-panic-mani.

is the point where I found myself shaking my head, because the theory that Will is trying to formulate here already exists in First Amendment theory. Specifically, it's what Thomas Emerson articulates in the scholarly writing that John Samples drew upon for his essay. And it's what Kate Klonick draws upon when she cites Jack Balkin's law-review article (which criticized the limitations of the Meiklejohnian politics-centric view of the First Amendment). As both Emerson and Balkin demonstrate, there's no need to reinvent the wheel when it comes to harmonizing free-speech theory with individual human needs. Contrary to Will's suggestion, Balkin does not "appeal to the authority of democracy to say that individuals should have a say in the development of culture." Instead, he's saying that participation in the development of culture just is a part of democracy, drawing not least upon the First Amendment theory underpinning our two-decade-old victory in the Supreme Court case *Reno v. ACLU* (1997)—a case that's still a triumph, it must be said, of pragmatic optimism.

I can't help finding myself wishing, after reading and rereading Will's contributions, to find stronger defenses of democracy, of freedom of expression, and of social media than the ones he offers us. It seems clear that Will doesn't think much of democracy itself. (He's right that we need to value "expertise," but the idea that voters need to be informed and have something to contribute to their governance is something he apparently accepts as a "folk theory of democracy.") And it seems just as clear that he thinks freedom of expression in social media doesn't mean much. He feels compelled to elaborate on his earlier declaration that "What people do online is engage in the pointless babble that is so often derided." In his follow-up essay, Will allows (without expressly admitting) that his generalization may apply only to "most" people. And he clarifies that the "pointless babble" isn't, strictly speaking, "pointless," since "these gestures are simply an example of what linguists call 'phatic communication.' " In other words, social media expression is not totally pointless because it might amount to communications like grunting or nodding to signal your shared presence with someone, or like saying "how's it going?" as a greeting when you're not really seeking factual declaration in response.

I don't think there's any serious dispute that some subset of social media expression is "phatic"—indeed, the early "poke" function on

Facebook was essentially nothing more than that. [245] Still, I don't think I'm in the grip of any "emancipatory vision" when I insist that actual, meaningful, valuable, non-phatic communication—including both political (Meiklejohnian) and cultural (Emersonian or Balkinian) take place every day on social media platforms. So in my view, defending social media and internet expression as "phatic communication," taken together with the implicit dismissal of the need for an informed citizenry as part of a "folk theory of democracy," strikes me as no defense at all.

---

245  Danica Radovanovic, *Phatic Posts: Even the Small Talk Can Be Big*, Sci. Am. Blog Network (Apr. 13, 2012), https://blogs.scientificamerican.com/guest-blog/phatic-posts-even-the-small-talk-can-be-big/.

CHAPTER 16

# If Facebook Is Really at War, the Only Way to Win Is to Put Ethics First

This article was originally published in *the Washington Post* on November 26, 2018, at https://www.washingtonpost.com/outlook/2018/11/26/if-facebook-is-really-war-only-way-win-is-put-ethics-first/.

Mark Zuckerberg has said he needs to be a "wartime" CEO[246] to respond to the cascade of public criticism that has swamped Facebook over the past two or three years. But a successful wartime leader can't focus just on defense or on diverting attacks elsewhere. Do Zuckerberg and Facebook have the kind of plan that would win back the trust of a more skeptical public or the respect of governments and the news media? It's unclear that they do, or even if they recognize that they lack one. But Facebook's current crisis of public confidence represents an opportunity to reshape the company's damaged relationships—if the company is willing to make some major changes.

Facebook doesn't seem ready for that. A *New York Times* report earlier this month[247] about the company's strategy of denial, delay

---

246   Casey Newton, *How Mark Zuckerberg became a wartime CEO*, The Verge (Nov. 20, 2018), https://www.theverge.com/2018/11/20/18103886/mark-zuckerberg-wartime-ceo-facebook-sheryl-sandberg.

247   Frenkel et al., *supra* note 1.

and deflection shows the company has been preoccupied with the "unfair" public criticism it has received—despite periodic declarations that Facebook recognizes it has maybe been doing some things wrong and plans to fix them. Zuckerberg offered some wan assurances in an interview with CNN last week, pledging that his company is reviewing "thousands of apps" with the goal of "making sure that developers like Aleksandr Kogan [author of the app used by Cambridge Analytica], who got access to a lot of information and then improperly used it, just don't get access to as much information going forward." Not as much access to information? That's weak sauce, and it doesn't sound at all like a comprehensive review of Facebook's strategic choices about how to handle our data.

Still, I get it. Like many other Facebook fans, I believe some significant percentage of the criticism leveled against the social network (that it's addictive, [248] for example, or that it puts us in "filter bubbles," [249] or that it makes us depressed [250]) are unfair and even silly. That's why I have been predisposed before to think the company's missteps are just ordinary new-medium growing pains.

But consider the reports that Facebook's strategic response to the criticism has included opposition research about the U.S. senators who would be quizzing Zuckerberg at his appearances before Congress this year. Facebook's departing public-policy chief Elliot Schrage more or less admitted as much in a blog post Wednesday, [251] characterizing the work of Definers Public Affairs and other firms Facebook has worked with as "useful to help respond to unfair claims where Facebook has been singled out for criticism, and to positively distinguish us from competitors." That's an awfully positive spin on efforts to spread the blame for Russian disinformation to tech rivals such as Google. (There was even a brain-dead effort to blame liberal philanthropist George Soros, a bête noire in the eyes of right-wing politicians, for the nonprofit organizations that have condemned some of the company's practices.)

---

248  Harris, *supra* note 1.

249  Jacob Weisberg, *Eli Pariser's The Filter Bubble: Is Web personalization turning us into solipsistic twits?*, Slate (June 10, 2011), https://slate.com/news-and-politics/2011/06/eli-pariser-s-the-filter-bubble-is-web-personalization-turning-us-into-solipsistic-twits.html.

250  Godwin, *supra* note 7.

251  *Elliot Schrage on Definers,* Facebook Newsroom (Nov. 21, 2018), http://newsroom.fb.com/news/2018/11/elliot-schrage-on-definers/.

This stuff happened, Schrage hints, because Facebook's relationship with Definers had become "less centrally managed."

Facebook has been making life particularly hard on those of us who have defended the company. I still see Facebook's major accomplishment in connecting more than 2 billion people as mostly positive. This doesn't mean I'm naively dismissing how the platform has been (mis)used mischievously and maliciously. I'm just not surprised by this misuse—which every new mass medium has experienced, starting with the printing press.

But the *Times* report, as well as follow-up coverage in the *Wall Street Journal*, make me more skeptical about Facebook's willingness to recognize its need to change. Is Facebook's use of Definers Public Affairs really just a recent lapse, given that the company engaged in a similar "defining" effort in 2011, when its leadership sought to blunt Google's efforts to start a competing social network? Facebook ultimately won out there, even though its rank tactic[252] was exposed by tech bloggers.

Still, Zuckerberg and Facebook absolutely do have the capacity to turn this crisis around, provided the company takes some aggressively forward-looking, positive steps.

Facebook needs to stop treating critics—even the meanest, most unfair and most intractable ones—as combatants. That's an unforced error that is centrally responsible for how bad the company looked after the *Times* article was published. Facebook is never going to win the hearts and minds of every critic, but the company may win over enough if it shows that it is listening to them and then makes significant changes in how it treats user data and speech.

Zuckerberg also should embrace the model of Facebook as an "information fiduciary"—an enterprise that has the same kinds of ethical obligations to users that lawyers have to clients or that doctors have to patients. That would mean not merely that Facebook is being more humane to its users—it also would help the company step up to the role of user advocate. There's a lot of good scholarship on this issue, notably from my colleague Jack Balkin at Yale Law School,[253] and it

---

252   Dan Lyons, *Facebook Busted in Clumsy Smear Attempt on Google*, Daily Beast (May 12, 2011), https://www.thedailybeast.com/facebook-busted-in-clumsy-smear-attempt-on-google.

253   Jack M. Balkin, *Information Fiduciaries and the First Amendment*, 49 UC Davis L. Rev. 1183 (2016), https://lawreview.law.ucdavis.edu/issues/49/4/Lecture/49-4'Balkin.pdf.

boils down to adopting fiduciary duties such as the duty of care, the duty of confidentiality and the duty of loyalty. In nonlawyer language, this means not being negligent with users' information, keeping it private, and not using users' information to serve the company's interest at the expense of users' well-being. This includes not leveraging data with the aim of controlling users or allowing third parties to do so. (This could have an ancillary effect of reducing "fake news," which is designed to play on readers' prejudices and fears.)

Being an information fiduciary means making a long-term unbreakable commitment. It's a set of obligations that sits on top of, and governs, the company's terms-of-service agreements with users.

Finally, the company ought to cease hostilities with its occasional rivals such as Apple and Google—even when they're critical of what Facebook has done. If the social network embraces the "information fiduciary" model, either it will have a competitive advantage against companies that don't embrace it, or the other companies will embrace it, too. An industry-wide adoption of fiduciary standards is a good answer to those critics, such as European Union regulators, who think American tech companies don't honor privacy enough. [254]

There are other advantages to adopting this stronger ethical framework in dealing with user information. Facebook may not have committed itself to being an advocate of user privacy against governments yet, but Google [255] and Apple [256] certainly have. The company definitely cares about telling users, to the extent possible, about how it handles government requests and demands. But status as an information fiduciary would give Facebook stronger standing to resist turning over user information in response to government demands—both from the U.S. government and from other governments that may have fewer due-process constraints. It also would put Facebook in the position of being advocates or even

---

254   Alex Hern, *Privacy policies of tech giants "still not GDPR-compliant"*, The Guardian (July 4, 2018), https://www.theguardian.com/technology/2018/jul/05/privacy-policies-facebook-amazon-google-not-gdpr-compliant.

255   Katie Hafner & Matt Richtel, *Google Resists U.S. Subpoena of Search Data*, N.Y. Times (Jan. 20, 2006), https://www.nytimes.com/2006/01/20/technology/google-resists-us-subpoena-of-search-data.html.

256   Sam Blum, *Apple just Made Its Phones Impossible For Police to Hack*, Popular Mechanics (Oct. 25, 2018), https://www.popularmechanics.com/technology/security/a24219241/apple-greykey-ios12-police-hacking/.

tribunes for user interests—in speech as well as privacy—if it wants to be. There's even some solid Supreme Court precedent [257] on this point.

The main thing for Zuckerberg and Facebook to remember is that, if they're going to assume a "wartime" footing to respond to a current crisis, they need to have a plan for the peace. That plan can't excuse any lapses of their earlier responsibilities toward users and toward society generally. Instead, Facebook needs to be more ambitious and promulgate new, higher standards of fiduciary duties to all of us. Other tech companies need to do this, too. That's what "wartime" CEO Mark Zuckerberg should aim for, and it's what a lasting peace requires.

257   *Patterson*, 357 U.S. 449.

## PART IV

# The Past and Future of Free Speech

# CHAPTER 17

# Looking Forward to the Next 20 Years of a Post-*Reno* Internet

This article was originally published in *Techdirt* on June 29, 2017, at https://www.techdirt.com/articles/20170628/17304937691/looking-forward-to-next-20-years-post-reno-internet.shtml.

The internet we have today could have been very different, more like the over-the-air broadcast networks that still labor under broad federal regulatory authority while facing declining relevance.

But 20 years ago this week, the United States made a different choice when the U.S. Supreme Court handed down its 9-0 opinion in *Reno v. ACLU*, [258] the case that established how fundamental free-speech principles like the First Amendment apply to the internet.

I think of *Reno* as "my case" because I'd been working toward First Amendment protections for the internet since my first days as a lawyer—the first staff lawyer for the Electronic Frontier Foundation (EFF), which

---

258    Tim Cushing, *How The ACLU's Fight To Protect "Indecent" Speech Saved The Internet From Being Treated Like Broadcast TV*, Techdirt (June 27, 2017), https://www.techdirt.com/articles/20170626/16543937676/how-aclus-fight-to-protect-indecent-speech-saved-internet-being-treated-like-broadcast-tv.shtml.

was founded in 1990 by software entrepreneur Mitch Kapor and Grateful Dead lyricist John Perry Barlow. There are other lawyers and activists who feel the same possessiveness about the *Reno* case, most with justification. What we all have in common is the sense that, with the Supreme Court's endorsement of our approach to the internet as a free-expression medium, we succeeded in getting the legal framework more or less right.

We had argued that the internet—a new, disruptive and, to some large extent, unpredictable medium—deserved not only the free-speech guarantees of the traditional press, but also the same freedom of speech that each of us has as an individual. The *Reno* decision established that our government has no presumptive right to regulate internet speech. The federal government and state governments can limit free speech on the internet only in narrow types of cases, consistent with our constitutional framework. As Chris Hanson, the brilliant ACLU lawyer and advocate who led our team, recently put it: "We wanted to be sure the internet had the same strong First Amendment standards as books, not the weaker standards of broadcast television." [259]

The decision also focused on the positive benefits this new medium had already brought to Americans and to the world. As one of the strategists for the case, I'd worked to frame this part of the argument with some care. I'd been a member of the Whole Earth 'Lectronic Link (the WELL) for more than five years and of many hobbyist computer forums (we called them bulletin-board systems or "BBSes") for a dozen years. In these early online systems—the precursors of today's social media like Facebook and Twitter—I believed I saw something new, a new form of community that encompassed both shared values and diversity of opinion. A few years before *Reno v. ACLU*—when I was a relatively young, newly minted lawyer—I'd felt compelled to try to figure out how these new communities work [260] and how they might interact with traditional legal understandings in American law, including the "community standards" [261] relevant to obscenity law and broadcasting law.

---

259   Noa Yachot, *The Magna Carta of Cyberspace Turns 20: An Interview With the ACLU Lawyer Who Helped Save the Internet*, Am. C.L. Union (June 23, 2017), https://www.aclu.org/blog/free-speech/internet-speech/magna-carta-cyberspace-turns-20-interview-aclu-lawyer-who-helped.

260   Mike Godwin, *Nine Principles for Making Virtual Communities Work*, Wired (June 1, 1994), https://www.wired.com/1994/06/vc-principles/.

261   Mike Godwin, *The Law: Virtual Community Standards*, Reason.com (Nov. 1,

When EFF, ACLU and other organizations, companies, and individuals came together to file a constitutional challenge to the Communications Decency Act that President Bill Clinton signed as part of the Telecommunications Act of 1996, not everyone on our team saw this issue the way I did, at the outset. Hanson freely admits that "[w]hen we decided to bring the case, none of [ACLU's lead lawyers] had been online, and the ACLU did not have a website." Hanson had been skeptical of the value of including testimony about what we now call "social media" but more frequently back then referred to as "virtual communities." As he puts it:

> I proposed we drop testimony about the WELL—the social media site—on the grounds that the internet was about the static websites, not social media platforms where people communicate with each other. I was persuaded not to do that, and since I was monumentally wrong, I'm glad I was persuaded.

Online communities turned out to be vastly more important than many of the lawyers first realized. The internet's potential to bring us together meant just as much as the internet's capacity to publish dissenting, clashing and troubling voices. Justice John Paul Stevens, who wrote the *Reno* opinion, came to understand that community values were at stake, as well. In early sections of his opinion, Justice Stevens dutifully reasons through traditional "community standards" law, as would be relevant to obscenity and broadcasting cases. He eventually arrives at a conclusion that acknowledges that a larger community is threatened by broad internet-censorship provisions:

> We agree with the District Court's conclusion that the CDA places an unacceptably heavy burden on protected speech, and that the defenses do not constitute the sort of "narrow tailoring" that will save an otherwise patently invalid unconstitutional provision. In *Sable*, 492 U. S., at 127, we remarked that the speech restriction at issue there amounted to "burn[ing] the house to roast the pig." The CDA, casting a far darker shadow over free speech, threatens to torch a large segment of the Internet community.

1994), https://reason.com/archives/1994/11/01/virtual-community-standards.

The opinion's recognition of "the Internet community" paved the way for the rich and expressive, but also divergent and sometime troubling internet speech and expression we have today.

Which leaves us with the question: now that we've had two decades of experience under a freedom-of-expression framework for the internet—one that has informed not just how we use the internet in the United States but also how other voices around the world use it—what do we now need to do to promote "the Internet community"?

In 2017, not everyone views the internet as an unalloyed blessing. Most recently, we've seen concern about whether Google facilitates copyright infringement, [262] whether Twitter's political exchanges are little more than "outrage porn" [263] and whether Facebook enables "hate speech." [264] U.K. Prime Minister Theresa May, who is almost exactly the same age I am, seems to view the internet primarily as an enabler of terrorism. [265]

Even though we're now a few decades into the internet revolution, my view is that it's still too early to make the call that the internet needs more censorship and government intervention. Instead, we need more protection of the free expression and online communities that we've come to expect. Part of that protection may come from some version of the network neutrality principles [266] currently being debated at the Federal Communications Commission, although it may not be the version in place under today's FCC rules.

In my view, there are two additional things the internet community needs now. The first is both legal and technological guarantees of privacy, including through strong encryption. The second is universal access—including for lower-income demographics and populations in underserved

---

262  Taplin, *supra* note 1.

263  Damon Linker, *Twitter is destroying America*, The Week (June 2, 2017), https://theweek.com/articles/702389/twitter-destroying-america.

264  Steven Rosenbaum, *The Internet, Hate Speech And Politics*, Forbes (Nov. 14, 2016), https://www.forbes.com/sites/stevenrosenbaum/2016/11/14/the-internet-hate-speech-and-politics/.

265  Andrew Griffin, *Theresa Mays internet plans could make it easier for terrorists, campaign group warns*, The Independent (June 5, 2017), https://www.independent.co.uk/life-style/gadgets-and-tech/news/london-attack-theresa-may-internet-regulation-terrorist-networks-jihadis-surveillance-privacy-a7773021.html.

266  Cecilia Kang, *F.C.C. Chairman Pushes Sweeping Changes to Net Neutrality Rules*, N.Y. Times (Apr. 26, 2017), https://www.nytimes.com/2017/04/26/technology/net-neutrality.html.

areas and developing countries—that would enable everyone to particulate fully, not just as consumers but also as contributors to our shared internet. For me, the best way to honor the 40th anniversary of *Reno v. ACLU* will be to make sure everybody is here on the internet to celebrate it.

# CHAPTER 18

# One Year After Charlottesville's "Unite the Right" Riots: Following Karl Popper, We Should Tolerate Intolerance, Within Reason

This article was originally published in *Libertarianism.org* on August 9, 2018, at https://www.libertarianism.org/prototype/one-year-after-charlottesvilles-unite-right-riots-following-karl-popper-we-should-tolerate. This is an excerpt from a longer original article.

Should digital censorship of hate speech be the default expectation and the default response?

This policy question can be distinguished from the question of whether Facebook, Twitter, et al., can or should sometimes curate users' speech and expression in furtherance of the platforms' policies. Certainly digital platforms like Facebook are within their rights to censor white-nationalist content or other hateful speech—we crafted Section

230 of the Communications Decency Act [267] precisely to enable such post-hoc self-policing by platforms without incurring legal liability for doing so. As a free-speech advocate, I wasn't particularly troubled when Facebook started blocking[268] posts with links to the *Daily Stormer*—the neo-Nazi website that helped organize the Charlottesville rally—unless you were condemning them in the same post. That said, I've written elsewhere that almost any platform-based censorship—imposed by a private entity upon public discourse—is certain to leave some large fraction of a platform's users unhappy, [269] insisting that the platform has gone too far or not far enough.

But I was slightly more troubled by actions taken by other internet companies that operate on a "different level of the stack." [270] It turns out that in the digital age, you don't need bricks and baseball bats to silence people. GoDaddy[271] and Google[272] cancelled the *Daily Stormer's* domain registrations, and Cloudflare terminated [273] their contract. While all of these companies are well within their legal rights to terminate their services, their actions raise some disturbing questions[274] for our norms associated with free speech in a democratic society. It's not a perfect analogy (no analogy is, really), but it's as if we punished hate speech by denying hate speakers the right to subscribe to a telephone service.

Leave aside the question of whether white nationalists deserve to suffer some kind of karmic justice for fomenting hate (it's hard to

267  47 U.S.C. § 230.

268  Casey Newton, *Facebook is deleting links to a viral attack on a Charlottesville victim*, The Verge (Aug. 14, 2017), https://www.theverge.com/2017/8/14/16147126/facebook-delete-viral-post-charlottesville-daily-stormer.

269  Godwin, *supra* note 2.

270  *Protocol stack*, Wikipedia (last edited Jan. 29, 2019), https://en.wikipedia.org/wiki/Protocol'stack.

271  *Daily Stormer being dumped by GoDaddy*, CBS News (Aug. 14, 2017), https://www.cbsnews.com/news/daily-stormer-being-dumped-by-godaddy-apparently-seized-by-anonymous/.

272  *Google cancels Neo-Nazi site registration soon after it was dumped by GoDaddy*, Cnbc (Aug. 14, 2017), https://www.cnbc.com/2017/08/14/godaddy-boots-the-daily-stormer-because-of-what-it-wrote-about-charlottesville-victim.html.

273  Matthew Prince, *Why We Terminated Daily Stormer*, Cloudflare (Aug. 16, 2017), https://blog.cloudflare.com/why-we-terminated-daily-stormer/.

274  Jeremy Malcolm et al., *Fighting Neo-Nazis and the Future of Free Expression*, Electronic Frontier Foundation (Aug. 17, 2017), https://www.eff.org/deeplinks/2017/08/fighting-neo-nazis-future-free-expression.

argue that they don't). The fact is, in an open society abiding by rule-of-law norms, we normally require due process before we take away the fundamental rights of even the most noxious dissident speakers. And speaking—even to large audiences, as the Klansmen in the Brandenburg case did—is a fundamental right under our system. It's true that free speech rights on today's internet are more typically mediated by private companies like Facebook and Twitter. (And, as a practical matter, they also can be facilitated or delimited by companies providing domain-name services or content-delivery networks.) Still, we ought to expect, and maybe require, that new limits on constitutional rights in the digital world will be the product of a deliberative democratic process, rather than the fact that some Nazis succeeded in getting under [Cloudflare CEO] Matthew Prince's skin.

In Popper's view, tolerance even of intolerant philosophies should be the rule as long as we can keep them in check through other means. As the Cato Institute's Jason Kuznicki has explained, [275] the preferred first response is through "rational argument" or democratic consensus. [The latter is what Popper in his discussion of "the paradox of tolerance" in *The Open Society and Its Enemies* calls "public opinion."]

Of course, shaping public opinion may present new challenges in the social media age. "Filter bubbles," increasing polarization, "fake news," and viral conspiracy theories have all been cited as reasons to conscript platforms to take a heavier hand in censoring certain kinds of speech, or groups of speakers. I've written about those demands a lot lately, notably here [276] and here. [277] I'm on the record as being more skeptical about "filter bubbles" than most. On the one hand, I think the problem of cherrypicking facts to support your views predates the internet. On the other, I think the predisposition of human beings to get into arguments on the internet undercuts the notion, that we just want to hear what confirms our opinions. (A version of this notion, advanced by law professor Cass Sunstein among others, argues that

---

275    Jason Kuznicki, *On the Paradox of Tolerance*, Libertarianism.org (Aug. 17, 2017), https://www.libertarianism.org/columns/paradox-tolerance.

276    Mike Godwin, *Has Facebook Merely Been Exploited By Our Enemies? Or Is Facebook Itself The Real Enemy?*, Techdirt (June 5, 2018), https://www.techdirt.com/articles/20180531/14372939953/has-facebook-merely-been-exploited-our-enemies-is-facebook-itself-real-enemy.shtml.

277    Godwin, *supra* note 12.

we're predisposed to hide in "information cocoons.") [278] To be clear, I agree that polarization and fake news—on social-media platforms as well as in traditional media—are problems. But these problems don't entail a solution that imposes censorship obligations on social-media platforms (or elsewhere in the stack) and then simply trusts those private companies to censor content for us. If you believe freedom of speech and the rule of law are central values of an open society, you shouldn't choose a cure that kills the disease by crippling the patient.

The most effective responses to violent ideologies, when it comes to marginalizing or defeating doctrines of hate, still has to be in "the public square"—sometimes the literal square and sometimes the public square that is public debate on social media. The literal public square is still sometimes the right place to congregate in opposition to intolerance. As David Cole, the ACLU's national legal director, pointed out in the *New York Review of Books*, [279] the white supremacists who called a rally in Boston the week after Charlottesville were "vastly outnumbered by tens of thousands of counter protesters who peacefully marched through the streets" to express their opposition to the white supremacists' views. Per Cole, "Free speech, in short, is exposing white supremacists' ideas to the condemnation they deserve."

Sometimes the public square will be Facebook or Twitter or some other current platform, or some new platform that hasn't even been rolled out yet.

Cole's right about how free speech works, which means our first takeaway, from a close reading of both our First Amendment framework and the philosopher who personified commitment to open societies, is to begin by taking the risk of being tolerant. This doesn't have to be our only response or our ultimate response. It just has to be our first response to intolerant speech. If we begin by tolerating the expression of intolerant views, we have the advantage. Intolerance, articulated openly and precisely, puts itself right in our critical crosshairs.

We know that when intolerance is out there, making itself known and earning (appropriate) condemnation, its weaknesses and shallowness

---

278   Brendan Nyhan, *Americans Dont Live in Information Cocoons*, N.Y. Times (Oct. 24, 2014), https://www.nytimes.com/2014/10/25/upshot/americans-dont-live-in-information-cocoons.html.

279   David Cole, *Why We Must Still Defend Free Speech*, N.Y. Rev. Books (Sept. 28, 2017), https://www.nybooks.com/articles/2017/09/28/why-we-must-still-defend-free-speech/.

and illogic becomes self-evident rather than covert. And when that intolerance is openly expressed, we can't and mustn't passively accept the First Amendment's protection of intolerant thought. Instead, we know our first duty as members of an open society is to exercise our own First Amendment rights to challenge intolerance and refute it.

CHAPTER 19

# The Splinters of Our Discontent: A Review of *Network Propaganda*

This article was originally published in *Techdirt* on January 18, 2019, at https://www.techdirt.com/articles/20190117/15361941413/splinters-our-discontent-review-network-propaganda.shtml.

Years before most of us thought Donald Trump would have a shot at the presidency, the Cato Institute's Julian Sanchez put a name on a problem he saw in American conservative intellectual culture. Sanchez called it "epistemic closure," [280] and he framed the problem this way:

One of the more striking features of the contemporary conservative movement is the extent to which it has been moving toward epistemic closure. Reality is defined by a multimedia array of interconnected and cross promoting conservative blogs, radio programs, magazines, and of course, Fox News. Whatever conflicts with that reality can be dismissed out of hand because it comes from the liberal media, and is therefore ipso facto not to be trusted. (How do you know they're liberal? Well, they disagree

---

280   Julian Sanchez, *Frum, Cocktail Parties, and the Threat of Doubt* (Mar. 26, 2010), http://www.juliansanchez.com/2010/03/26/frum-cocktail-parties-and-the-threat-of-doubt/.

with the conservative media!) This epistemic closure can be a source of solidarity and energy, but it also renders the conservative media ecosystem fragile.

Sanchez's comments didn't trigger any kind of real schism in conservative or libertarian circles. Sure, there was some heated debate among conservatives, [281] and a few conservative commentators, like David Frum, Bruce Bartlett, and the *National Review*'s Jim Manzi, [282] acknowledged that there might be some merit to Sanchez's critique. But for most people, this argument among conservatives about epistemic closure hardly counted as serious news.

But the publication last fall of *Network Propaganda: Manipulation, Disinformation, and Radicalization in American Politics* by Yochai Benkler, Robert Faris, and Hal Roberts [283]—more than eight years after the original "epistemic closure" debate erupted—ought to make the issue hot again. This long, complex, yet readable study of the American media ecosystem in the run-up to the 2016 election (as well as the year afterwards) demonstrates that the epistemic-closure problem has generated what the authors call an "epistemic crisis" for Americans in general. The book also shows that our efforts to understand current political division and disruptions simplistically—either in terms of negligent and arrogant platforms like Facebook, or in terms of Bond-villain malefactors like Cambridge Analytica or Russia's Internet Research Agency—are missing the forest for the trees. It's not that the social media platforms are wholly innocent, and it's not that the would-be warpers of voter behavior did nothing wrong (or had no effect). But the seeds of the unexpected outcomes in the 2016 U.S. elections, *Network Propaganda* argues, were planted decades earlier, with the rise of a right-wing media ecosystem that valued loyalty and confirmation of conservative (or "conservative") values and narratives over truth.

---

281   Patricia Cohen, *'Epistemic Closure?' Those Are Fighting Words for Conservatives*, N.Y. Times (Jan. 3, 2016), https://www.nytimes.com/2010/04/28/books/28conserv.html.

282   Jim Manzi, *Liberty and Tyranny and Epistemic Closure*, National Review (Apr. 21, 2010), https://www.nationalreview.com/corner/liberty-and-tyranny-and-epistemic-closure-jim-manzi/.

283   Yochai Benkler et al., Network Propaganda: Manipulation, Disinformation, and Radicalization in American Politics (2018).

Now, if you're a conservative, you may be reading this broad characterization of *Network Propaganda* as an attack on conservatism itself. Here are four reasons you shouldn't fall into that trap! First, nothing in this book challenges what might be called core conservative values (at least as they have been understood for most of the last 100 years or so). Those values typically have included favoring limited government over expansive government, preferring economic growth and rights to property over promoting equity and equality for their own sake, supporting business flexibility over labor and governmental demands, committing to certain approaches to tax policy, and so forth. Nothing in *Network Propaganda* is a criticism of substantive conservative values like these, or even of what may increasingly be taken as "conservative" stances in the Trump era (nationalism or protectionism or opposition to immigration, say). The book doesn't take a position on traditional liberal or progressive political stances either.

Second, nothing in the book discounts the indisputable fact that individuals and media entities on the left, and even in the center, have their own sins and excesses to account for. In fact, the more damning media criticisms in the book are aimed squarely at the more traditional journalistic institutions that made themselves more vulnerable to disinformation and distorted narratives in the name of "objectivity." Where right-wing media set out to reinforce conservative identity and narratives—doing, in fact, what they more or less always promised they were going to do—the institutional press of the left and the center frequently let their superficial commitment to objectivity result in the amplification of disinformation and distortions.

Third, there are philosophical currents on the left as well as the right that call the whole notion of objective facts and truth into question—that consider all questions of fact to represent political judgments rather than anything that might be called "factual" or "truthful." As the authors put it, reform of our media ecosystems "will have to overcome not only right-wing propaganda, but also decades of left-wing criticism of objectivity and truth-seeking institutions." Dedication to truth-seeking is, or ought to be, a transpartisan [284] value.

Which leads us to the fourth reason conservatives should pay attention to *Network Propaganda*, which is the biggest one. The progress of knowledge, and of problem-solving in the real world, requires us,

---

284   *Transpartisan*, Wikipedia (last edited Aug. 26, 2018), https://en.wikipedia.org/wiki/Transpartisan.

regardless of political preferences and philosophical approaches, to come together in recognizing the value of facts. Consider: if progressives had cocooned themselves in a media ecosystem that had cut itself from the facts—that valued tribal loyalty and shared identity over mere factual accuracy—conservatives and centrists would be justified in pointing out not merely that the left's media were unmoored but also that its insistence on doctrinal purity in the face of factual disproof was positively destructive.

But the massive dataset and analyses offered by Benkler, Faris, and Roberts in *Network Propaganda* demonstrate persuasively that the converse distortion has happened. Specifically, the authors took about four million online stories regarding the 2016 election or national politics generally and analyzed them through Media Cloud, a joint technological project developed by Harvard's Berkman Klein Center and MIT's Center for Civil Media over the course of the last decade. Media Cloud enabled the authors to study not only where the stories originate but also how they were linked and propagated, and how the various entities in our larger media ecosystem link to one another. The Media Cloud analytical system made it possible to study news sites, including the website versions of newspapers like the *New York Times* and the *Wall Street Journal*, along with the more politically focused websites on the left and right, like Daily Kos and Breitbart. The system also enabled the authors to study how the stories were retweeted and shared on Facebook, Twitter, and other social media, as well as how, in particular instances, television coverage supplemented or amplified online stories.

You might expect that any study of such a large dataset would show symmetrical patterns of polarization during the pre-election to post-election period the authors studied (basically, 2015 through 2017). It was, after all, an election period, which is typically a time of increased partisanship. You might also expect, given the increasing presence of social-media platforms like Facebook, Twitter, and Instagram in American public life, that the new platforms themselves, just by their very existence and popularity, shaped public opinion in new ways. And you might expect, given the now-indisputable fact that Russian "active measures" [285] were trying to influence the American electorate in certain ways, to see clear proof either that the Russians succeeded in their disinformation/propaganda efforts (or that they failed).

285  *Active Measures*, Wikipedia (last edited Feb. 9, 2019), https://en.wikipedia.org/wiki/Active·measures.

Yet *Network Propaganda*, instantly a necessary text for those of us who study media ecologies, shows that the data point to different conclusions. The authors' Media Cloud analyses (frequently represented visually in colorful graphs as well as verbally in tables and in the text of the book itself) point to different conclusions altogether. As Benkler characterizes the team's findings in the *Boston Review*:

> The data was not what we expected. There were periods during the research when we were just working on identifying—as opposed to assessing—the impact of Russians, and during those times, I thought it might really have been the Russians. But as we analyzed these millions of stories, looking both at producers and consumers, a pattern repeated again and again that had more to do with the traditional media than the Internet. [286]

That traditional media institutions are seriously culpable for the spread of disinformation is counterintuitive. The authors begin *Network Propaganda* by observing what most of us also observed—the rise of what briefly was called "fake news" before that term was transmuted by President Trump into shorthand for his critics. But Benkler et al. also note that that the latter half of the 20th century, mainstream journalistic institutions, informed by a wave of professionalization that dates back approximately to the founding of the Columbia University journalism school, historically had been able to overcome most of the fact-free calumnies and conspiracy theories through their commitment to objectivity and fact-checking. Yet mainstream journalism failed the culture in 2016, and it's important for the journals and the journalists to come to terms with why. But doing so means investigating how stories from the fringes interacted with the mainstream.

The fringe stories had weird staying power; in the period centering on the 2016 election, a lot of the stories that were just plain crazy—from the absurd narrative that was "Pizzagate" [287] to claims that Jeb Bush had "close Nazi ties" [288] (Alex Jones played a role in both of these narratives)—persistently resurfaced in the way citizens talked about the election. To

---

286  Yochai Benkler et al., *Selling Outrage*, Boston Rev. (Nov. 12, 2018), http://bostonreview.net/politics/yochai-benkler-deborah-chasman-selling-outrage.

287  *Pizzagate conspiracy theory*, Wikipedia (last edited Jan. 28, 2019), https://en.wikipedia.org/wiki/Pizzagate'conspiracy'theory.

288  Alex Jones, *Jeb Bush: Close Nazi Ties Exposed*, InfoWars (Dec. 16, 2015), https://www.infowars.com/jeb-bush-close-nazi-ties-exposed/.

the *Network Propaganda* authors, it became clear that in recent years something new has emerged—namely, a variety of disinformation that seems, weedlike, to survive the most assiduous fact-checkers and persist in resurfacing in the public mind.

How did this emergence happen, and should we blame the internet? Certainly this phenomenon didn't manifest in any way predicted by either the more optimistic pundits at the internet's beginnings or the backlash pessimists who followed. The optimists had believed that increased democratic access to mass media might give rise to a wave of citizen journalists who supplemented and ultimately complemented institutional journalism, leading both to more accuracy in reporting and more citizen engagement. The pessimists predicted "information cocoons" (Cass Sunstein's term [289]) and "filter bubbles" (Eli Pariser's term [290]) punctuated to some extent by quarrelsomeness because online media can act as disinhibition to bad behavior. [291]

Yes, to some extent, the optimists and the pessimists both found confirmation of their predictions, but what they didn't expect, and what few if any seem to have predicted, was the marked asymmetry of how the predictions played in the 2015–2017 period with regard to the 2016 election processes and their outcome. As the authors put it, "[t]he consistent pattern that emerges from our data is that, both during the highly divisive election campaign and even more so during the first year of the Trump presidency, there is no left-right division, but rather a division between the right and the rest of the media ecosystem. The right wing of the media ecosystem behaves precisely as the echo-chamber models predict—exhibiting high insularity, susceptibility to information cascades, rumor and conspiracy theory, and drift toward more extreme versions of itself. The rest of the media ecosystem, however, operates as an interconnected network anchored by organizations, both for profit and nonprofit, that adhere to professional journalistic norms."

As a result, this period saw the appearance of disinformation narratives that targeted Trump and his primary opponents as well as Hillary Clinton, but the narratives that got more play, not just in right-wing outlets but

---

289  Brendan Nyhan, *Americans Don't Live in Information Cocoons*, N.Y. Times (Oct. 24, 2014), https://www.nytimes.com/2014/10/25/upshot/americans-dont-live-in-information-cocoons.html.

290  *Filter bubble, supra* note 9.

291  *Online Disinhibition Effect*, Wikipedia (last edited Feb. 22, 2019), https://en.wikipedia.org/wiki/Online_disinhibition_effect.

ultimately in the traditional journalistic outlets as well, were the ones that centered on Clinton. This happened even when there were fewer available facts supporting the anti-Clinton narratives and (occasionally) more facts supporting the anti-Trump narratives. The explanation for the anti-Clinton narratives' longevity in the news cycle, the data show, is the focus of the right-wing media ecology on the two focal media nodes of Fox News and Breitbart. At times during this period, Breitbart took the lead as an influencer from Fox News, which eventually responded by repositioning itself after Trump's nomination as a solid Trump booster.

In contrast, left-wing media had no single outlet that defined orthodoxy for progressives. Instead, left-of-center outlets worked within the larger sphere of traditional media, and, because they were competing for the rest of the audience that had not committed itself to the Fox/Breitbart ecosystem, were constrained to adhere, mostly, to facts that were confirmable by traditional media institutions associated with the center-left (the *New York Times* and the *Washington Post*, say) as well as with the center-right (e.g., the *Wall Street Journal*). Basically, even if you were an agenda-driven left-oriented publication or online outlet, your dependence on reaching the mainstream for your audience meant that, you couldn't get away with just making stuff up, or with laundering far-left conspiracy theories from more marginal sources.

*Network Propaganda*'s data regarding the right-wing media ecosystem—that it's insular, prefers confirmation of identity and loyalty rather than self-correction, demonizes perceived opponents, and resists disconfirmation of its favored narratives—map well to social-science political-communication theorists Kathleen Hall Jamieson and Joseph Capella's 2008 book, *Echo Chamber: Rush Limbaugh and the Rise of Conservative Media.* [292] In that book, Jamieson and Capella outlined how, as they put it, "these conservative media create a self-protective enclave hospitable to conservative beliefs." As a consequence, they write:

> This safe haven reinforces conservative values and dispositions, holds Republican candidates and leaders accountable to conservative ideals, tightens their audience's ties to the Republican Party, and distances listeners, readers, and viewers from "liberals," in general, and Democrats, in particular. It also enwraps them in a

---

292   Kathleen Hall Jamieson & Joseph N. Cappella, Echo Chamber: Rush Limbaugh and the Conservative Media Establishment (2008).

world in which facts supportive of Democratic claims are contested and those consistent with conservative ones championed.

The data analyzed by Benkler et al. in *Network Propaganda* support
Jamieson's and Capella's conclusions from more than a decade ago.
Moreover, Benkler et al. argue that the key factors in the promotion
of disinformation were not "clickbait fabricators" (who generate eye-
grabbing headlines to generate revenue), or Russian "active measures,"
or the corrosive effects of the (relatively) new social-media platforms
Facebook and Twitter. The authors are aware that in making this argument
they're swimming against the tide:

> Fake news entrepreneurs, Russians, the Facebook algorithm,
> and online echo chambers provide normatively unproblematic,
> nonpartisan explanations to the current epistemic crisis. For all of
> these actors, the strong emphasis on technology suggests a novel
> challenge that our normal systems do not know how to handle
> but that can be addressed in a nonpartisan manner. Moreover,
> focusing on 'fake news' from foreign sources and on Russian
> efforts to intervene places the blame onto foreigners with no le-
> gitimate stake in our democracy. Both liberal political theory and
> professional journalism consistently seek neutral justifications
> for democratic institutions, so visibly nonpartisan explanations
> such as these have enormous attraction.

Nevertheless, *Network Propaganda* argues, the nonpartisan
explanations are inconsistent with what the data show, which the authors
characterize as "a radicalization of roughly a third of the American media
system." (It isn't "polarization," since the data don't show any symmetry
between left and right "poles.") The authors argue that "[n]o fact emerges
more clearly from our analysis of how four million political stories were
linked, tweeted, and shared over a three-year period than that there
is no symmetry in the architecture and dynamics of communications
within the right-wing media ecosystem and outside of it." In addition,
they write, "we have observed repeated public humiliation and vicious
disinformation campaigns mounted by the leading sites in this sphere
against individuals who were the core pillars of Republican identity a
mere decade earlier." Those campaigns against Republican stalwarts
came from the radicalized right-wing media sources, not from the left.

The authors acknowledge that they "do not expect our findings to persuade anyone who is already committed to the right-wing media ecosystem. [The data] could be interpreted differently. They could be viewed as a media system overwhelmed by liberal bias and opposed only by a tightly-clustered set of right-wing sites courageously telling the truth in the teeth of what Sean Hannity calls the 'corrupt, lying media,' rather than our interpretation of a radicalized right set apart form a media system anchored in century-old norms of professional journalism." But that interpretation of the data flies in the face of *Network Propaganda*'s extensive demonstration that the traditional mainstream media—in what the authors call "the performance of objectivity"—actually had the effect of amplifying right-wing narratives rather than successfully challenging the false or distorted narratives. (The authors explore this paradox in Chapter 6.)

Democrats and progressives won't have any trouble accepting the idea that radicalized right-wing media are the primary cause of what the authors call today's "epistemic crisis." But Benkler and his co-authors want Republicans to recognize what they lost in 2016:

> The critical thing to understand as you read this book is that the epochal change reflected by the 2016 election and the first year of the Trump presidency was not that Republicans beat Democrats [but instead] that in 2016 the party of Ronald Reagan and the two presidents Bush was defeated by the party of Donald Trump, Breitbart, and billionaire Robert Mercer. As our data show, in 2017 Fox News joined the victors in launching sustained attacks on core pillars of the Party of Reagan—free trade and a relatively open immigration policy, and, most directly, the national security establishment and law enforcement when these threatened President Trump himself.

It's possible that many or even most Republicans don't yet want to hear this message—the recent shuttering of *The Weekly Standard*[293] underscores one of the consequences of radicalization of right-wing media, which is that center-right outlets, more integrated with the mainstream media in terms of journalistic professionalism and factuality, have lost

---

293    Oliver Darcy, *The Weekly Standard, a Conservative Magazine Critical of Trump, to Shutter After 23 Years*, CNN (Dec. 14, 2018), https://www.cnn.com/2018/12/14/media/weekly-standard-end/index.html.

influence in the right-wing media sphere. (It remains to be seen whether *The Bulwark*[294] helps fill the gap.)

But the larger message from *Network Propaganda*'s analyses is that we're fooling ourselves if we blame our current culture's vulnerability to disinformation on the internet in general or on social media (or search engines, or smartphones) . . . or even on Russian propaganda campaigns. Blaming the Russians is trendy these days, and even Kathleen Jamieson, whose 2008 book on right-wing media, *Echo Chamber,*[295] informs the authors' work in *Network Propaganda*, has adopted the thesis that the Russians probably made the difference for Trump in 2016. Her recent book *Cyberwar*[296]—published a month after *Network Propaganda* was published—spells out a theory of Russian influence in the 2016 election that also, predictably, raises concerns about social media, as well as focusing on the role of the Wikileaks releases of hacked DNC emails and how the mainstream media responded to those releases.

Popular accounts of Jamieson's book have interpreted *Cyberwar* as proof that the Russians are the central culprits in any American 2016 electoral dysfunction, even though Jamieson carefully qualifies her reasoning and conclusions in all the ways you would want a responsible social scientist to do. (She doesn't claim to have proved her thesis conclusively.) Taken together with the trend of seeing social media as inherently socially corrosive, the Russians-did-it narrative suggests that if Twitter and Facebook (and Facebook-integrated platforms like Instagram and WhatsApp) clean up their acts and find ways to purge their products of foreign actors as well as homegrown misleading advertising and "fake news," the political divisiveness we've seen in recent years will subside. But *Network Propaganda* provides strong reason to believe that reforming or regulating or censoring the internet companies won't solve the problems they're being blamed for. True, the book expressly endorses public-policy responses to the disinformation campaigns of malicious foreign actors as well as reforms of how the platforms handle political advertising. But, the authors insist, the problem isn't primarily the Russians, or technology—it's in our political and media cultures.

---

294    Oliver Darcy, *Former Weekly Standard Staffers Find New Home at The Bulwark, a Conservative Site Unafraid to Take On Trump,* CNN (Jan. 4, 2019), https://www.cnn.com/2019/01/04/media/weekly-standard-the-bulwark/index.html.

295    Jamieson & Cappella, *supra* note 13.

296    Kathleen Hall Jamieson, Cyberwar: How Russian Hackers and Trolls Helped Elect a President What We Don't, Can't, and Do Know (2018).

Possibly Jamieson is right to think that the Russians' "active measures" were efforts that, amplifying pre-existing political divisions through social media, were the final straw that ultimately changed the outcome of the 2016 election. Nevertheless, at its best Jamieson's book has taken a snapshot of how vulnerable our political culture was in 2016. Plus, her theory of Russian influence requires some suspension of disbelief, notably in her theory about how then-FBI-director James Comey's interventions—departures from DOJ/FBI norms—were caused somehow by the fact of the Russian campaign. Even if you accept her account, it's an account of our vulnerability that doesn't explain where the vulnerability came from.

In contrast, *Network Propaganda* has a fully developed theory of where that vulnerability came from, and traces it—in ways aligned with Jamieson's previous scholarship—to sources that predate the modern internet and social media. In addition, in what may be a surprise given the book's focus on what might be mistakenly taken as a problem unique to American political culture, *Network Propaganda* expressly places the American problems in the context of the larger currents around the world to blame internet platforms in particular for social ills:

> For those not focused purely on the American public sphere, our study suggests that we should focus on the structural, not the novel; on the long-term dynamic between institutions, culture, and technology, not only the disruptive technological moment; and on the interaction between the different media and technologies that make up a society's media ecosystem, not on a single medium, like the internet, much less a single platform like Facebook or Twitter. The stark differences we observe between the insular right-wing media ecosystem and the majority of the American media environment, and the ways in which open web publications, social media, television, and radio all interacted to produce these differences, suggest that the narrower focus will lead to systematically erroneous predictions and diagnoses. It is critical not to confound what is easy to measure (Twitter) with what is significantly effective in shaping beliefs and politically actionable knowledge in society.... Different countries, with different histories, institutional structures, and cultural practices of collective sense-making need not fear the internet's effects. There is no echo chamber or filter-bubble effect that will inexorably take

a society with a well-functioning public sphere and turn it into a shambles simply because the internet comes to town.

Benkler, Faris, and Roberts expressly acknowledge, however, that it's appropriate for governments and companies to consider how they regulate political advertising and targeted messaging going forward—even if this online content can't be shown to have played a significant corrosive role in past elections, there's no guarantee that refined versions won't be more effective in the future. But even more important, they insist, is the need to address larger institutional issues affecting our public sphere. The book's Chapter 13 addresses a full range of possible reforms. These include "reconstructing center-right media" (to address what the authors think Julian Sanchez correctly characterized as an "epistemic closure" problem) as well as insisting that professional journalists recognize that they're operating in a propaganda-rich media culture, which ethically requires them to do something more than "performance of objectivity."

The recommendations also include promoting what they call a "public health approach to the media ecosystem," which essentially means obligating the tech companies and platforms to disclose "under appropriate legal constraints [such as protecting individual privacy]" the kind of data we need to assess media patterns, dysfunctions, and outcomes. They write, correctly, that we "can no more trust Facebook to be the sole source of information about the effects of its platform on our media ecosystem than we could trust a pharmaceutical company to be the sole source of research on the outcome of its drugs, or an oil company to be the sole source of measurements of particles emissions or $CO_2$ in the atmosphere."

The fact is that the problems in our political and media culture can't be delegated to Facebook or Twitter to solve on their own. Any comprehensive, holistic solutions to our epistemic crises require not only transparency and accountability but also fully engaged democracy with full access to the data. Yes, that means you and me. It's time for our epistemic opening.

CHAPTER 20

# Some Final Observations, Plus a Closing Argument

Some books are planned, and others arrive organically—which is the fancy way of saying by surprise. This is the latter kind of book. It's built around a series of articles I wrote over the last three years whose purpose was to make sense of the current moral panic about social media and tech companies—the "techlash" as the cool kids call it. Over the course of writing these pieces I began to recognize what seemed to me to be larger patterns, some of which reflect historically well-documented moral panics, while others signify a new dynamic of push-and-pull between internet technologies and internet polices. This chapter represents some speculations about how we got to where we are now and what we should do next about it.

In my first book, written a little more than twenty years ago, I'd written about what I saw as a "backlash" at the time. Why "backlash"? (Or "techlash"?) Mainly because, once again, a period of not-entirely-well-considered optimism was quickly followed by a much stronger sense of certainty that something about the internet and digital technology itself was antagonistic towards or corrosive of human happiness (or even sanity).

There are differences, of course. In the 1990s, the backlash, to the extent it was grounded in something real, was mostly concerned about digital pornography and digital copyright infringement. Unsurprisingly, then, the two major legislative changes in the United States to spin out of the 1990s backlash were the Communications Decency Act and the Digital Millennium Copyright Act. The CDA was challenged in court and mostly struck down, except for a provision whose central purpose was to enable internet services to censor bad content their users posted without automatically acquiring legal liability for the content they didn't censor or originate. My colleague Jeff Kosseff has just published a book on the CDA's Section 230s [297] that I think works well as a companion volume for the book you hold now in your hands. A second statute, the Digital Millennium Copyright Act, created a copyright-specific framework that enables internet services to respond effectively to complaints about copyright infringement—and to limit infringement—in ways that mostly avoid the need for anyone to go to court. The chief problem generated by the success of CDA 230 and the DMCA is that, for many younger lawyers and policymakers, they're perceived as the Big Bang of internet law—few students of these laws give attention to what actually preceded and gave rise to these two statutes. (Jeff's book is a corrective in this regard.)

Both CDA 230 and the DMCA have their critics, but they're generally regarded us internet lawyers as having created the environment that allows countless successful enterprises, from purely commercial enterprises like Google and Facebook and Twitter to purely philanthropic enterprises like Wikipedia, to flourish. The success of the commercial internet companies—in particular the U.S.-based ones—has been remarkable in recent years because the current market leaders have mostly dusted their competition. The market-dominant companies have made domestic regulators and policymakers nervous simply because of the power and capital they wield; they've made foreign and international regulators nervous because, in addition to their market leadership, they're mostly American enterprises. Even if the companies had made entirely thoughtful and well-considered decisions about how to regulate or moderate content on their sites—or about how to steward the personal information users left on their sites—the sheer scale of their operations would guarantee that lawmakers and regulators would raise questions about whether they were handling the power responsibly.

**How the companies' communications strategies fell short.** And of course the companies, to put it most charitably, have not always been responsible or thoughtful actors. Sometimes this has been due to ar-

---

297 Jeff Kosseff, The Twenty-Six Words That Created the Internet (2019).

rogance—as when Facebook assumed that, when it demanded that Cambridge Analytica destroy the data it had obtained from Facebook users in violation of its policies, the data truly were completely destroyed. (They weren't. [298]) To some extent it has been due to shortsightedness, as when Twitter's leadership assumed its protections under CDA 230 might mute criticism of the platform for not moderating more content, or for moderating content, as David Simon points out in Chapter 8, more for tone and invective than for actual factual falsity. I share Simon's disdain for policing civility and overlooking actual issues of falsehood. As he puts it, "It's as if they can't solve murders, robberies, and rapes in this town, so rather than confront the long and hard journey of real police work, the folks at Twitter are going to make this the least-jaywalkingest ville in Christendom." Certainly policing content for civility is orders of magnitude easier than policing it for factuality. Even so, my colleague Renee DiResta and I have some ideas about how the latter can be tailored to scale better on large platforms. [299]

The companies' stumbles on both content moderation and privacy have been grounded less in malice and profit motive than in arrogance and failure to listen to ideas that aren't their own. This attitude, which may even serve a purpose if one is starting up a paradigm-shifting commercial enterprise, doesn't translate well into the public-policy world, where recognizing and achieving consensus is more centrally important. This is something I began to understand better with a couple of case studies I embarked on in 2015, one involving Facebook in India and another centering on Uber and Lyft ride-hailing services in my home town, Austin, Texas. [300]

---

298    Kevin Granville, *Facebook and Cambridge Analytica: What You Need to Know as Fallout Widens*, N.Y. Times (Mar. 19, 2018), https://www.nytimes.com/2018/03/19/technology/facebook-cambridge-analytica-explained.html.

299    Such policing requires that the focus can't be on mere false statements—everybody says something false sometimes—but instead on deliberate disinformation. *See* Renee DiResta & Mike Godwin, *The Seven Step Program for Fighting Disinformation*, Just Security (Feb. 28, 2019), https://www.justsecurity.org/62718/step-program-fighting-disinformation/. This op-ed is also reproduced, with Renee's permission, as Appendix A at the end of this book. My lawyerly view is that "deliberate disinformation" can be understood in criminal-law or libel-law terms as "intentional" or "reckless" falsehood, a.k.a. "actual malice" in the language of the landmark Supreme Court libel case *New York Times*, 376 U.S. 254.

300    Mike Godwin, Catching the Third Wave: A Tale of Two Tech-Policy Battles (R St. Inst., Policy Study No. 72, Oct. 2016), https://2o9ub0417chl2lg6m43em6psi2i-wpengine.netdna-ssl.com/wp-content/uploads/2018/04/72-1.pdf.

Most of this book was written after the 2016 votes in the Brexit plebiscite and in the United States elections brought the question of whether social media were damaging to democracy to the foreground. But even a year or two those votes—in, respectively, June and November of 2016—it seemed clear to me that many of today's tech-company success stories might be headed for a reckoning. Specifically, Facebook's efforts in India to promote free-for-subscribers, "zero-rated" low-bandwidth applications led to a backlash by network-neutrality activists who, on the one hand, believed Facebook's initiative undermined net neutrality and, on the other hand, suspected that Facebook might imperialistically crowd out possible Indian competitors, not to mention misusing whatever private user data it gathered. These fears weren't wholly irrational, which meant that Facebook's task was to persuade its serious Indian critics of the overall benefits of its zero-rated platform (first known as "Internet. org" and later as "Free Basics"). On the merits, Facebook had some good arguments, and I wrote positively about those arguments in a Slate article in the fall of 2015. [301]

But when I went to India early in 2016, at the invitation of Pranesh Prakash of India's Center for Internet and Society, to speak about the issue and talk to stakeholders it became clear to me that Facebook was headed for a public-policy loss regardless of the merits of its arguments (and regardless of the lack of merit of some, although not all, of its critics' arguments). Over the course of a week, in Bangalore, Mumbai, and Delhi, I learned quickly that Facebook's full-court public-relations campaign for Free Basics was actively alienating potential allies and energizing its critics. In other words, its PR campaign was actually making things worse, and India's telecom-regulatory agency bowed to public pressure and effectively outlawed Free Basics—and probably any other similar effort to provide free internet resources to cash-strapped mobile users who otherwise will have to pay for more bits in their data plans.

I was so struck by Facebook's public-policy debacle in India—which to me seemed to speak of larger corporate-culture problems—that I started to write a case study about it. But just as I began that effort, the public campaign in Austin, Texas, over how the ride-hailing services Uber and Lyft would be regulated by the city was proceeding to its own

---

301   Mike Godwin, *Activists Criticized Facebook's Internet Project for Developing Nations. Facebook Listened*, Slate (Sept. 30, 2015), https://slate.com/technology/2015/09/facebooks-internet-org-is-now-free-basics-and-critics-should-love-it.html.

vote. Although the two public-policy debates were not precisely parallel (India's centered on a telecom-agency regulation, while Austin's turned on a public referendum about ride-sharing regulation), they had a lot in common. Principally, the companies threw money at the issue, and in both cases the public reacted badly to the implication that they could be bought. My case study of Facebook's campaign in India grew into a compare-and-contrast study in which I focused on lessons we might learn from what happened to Facebook in India and to Uber and Lyft in Austin. [302]

**How the companies' moderation strategies will continue to fall short.**
And to a very large extent the companies' bad decisions about moderating content come from their conviction that if a rich company like Facebook can just quickly develop the right combination of policies, enforced both by algorithm and by human intervention—and perhaps with some tweaking of platform features—it can innovate its way out of its problems and the criticisms those problems engender. That conviction turns out to be mistaken for a number of reasons. First and foremost, it assumes that content-moderation problems are tractable in a way that can be made to scale for a global platform—either through increased human intervention or innovative content-screen algorithms or both. That assumption is false because human communications are as subtle and tricky and nuanced and context-dependent as the minds that generate them. An algorithm that targets "hate speech," for example, may flag communications that quote hate speech in order to be critical of it. An online environment that's designed to support freedom of expression needs to accommodate expression that, while offensive in its original context, is usefully illustrative of a conceptual or social problem in another. Algorithms may be useful at flagging possible problems, but they're mostly not useful at reaching final judgment about them. Hiring legions of content moderators to make snap judgments about content not only may be actively harmful to moderators themselves, [303] but it also may be harmful to free speech itself, because human errors in judgment will inevitably occur. Furthermore, they give rise to unhap-

---

302   The paper can be found here as a downloadable PDF file: Godwin, *supra* note 4.

303   Casey Newton, *The secret lives of Facebook moderators in America*, The Verge (Feb. 25, 2019), https://www.theverge.com/2019/2/25/18229714/cognizant-facebook-content-moderator-interviews-trauma-working-conditions-arizona.

piness among users, who inevitably will detect and complain about inconsistencies and mistakes.

A simple solution might be to legally transmute the services and platforms into common carriers—actively barring companies like Facebook and Twitter from curating or blocking any content. But the short-term benefit of eliminating the inconsistencies and mistakes of algorithmic or human-based moderation will almost certainly be outweighed by the removal of any constraints on garbage content, ranging from disinformation to "hate speech" to doxing and publication of everyone's intimate or embarrassing photos (which themselves may be real or may be "deep fakes"). The purpose of CDA 230 was to enable moderators to fix problems they see without becoming legally liable for garbage content they didn't see, or misinterpreted or misclassified. An analogy may be useful here: if your town experiences a blizzard and the city's snowplow misses your street—or perhaps plows your street but damages your car or buries it in snow—that's not an argument for eliminating snowplows altogether. CDA 230 recognizes that the internet's streets need to be cleared, but builds in a recognition that, ultimately, it's human beings who are doing the clearing, and we don't want the perfect to be the enemy of the good and necessary.

So we have to give the internet companies some scope to moderate content—even though doing so means that there will always be critics who insist that the moderating is either too little, or too much, or just plain wrong. The fact that there will be critics is part of the human condition and therefore unavoidable, so we have to set our expectations accordingly. Facebook and Twitter aren't perfect, Google isn't perfect, digital technology itself isn't perfect, and there can be no perfect set of content decisions that will please everyone. We need to learn to recognize and accept all that imperfection. [304]

That recognition is not where we are now, however. And part of the problem is that our governments—not just the United States but also

---

304   It may reasonably be argued that the market dominance of a few platforms and services means that we can't rely on market competition to incentivize the companies to improve their content moderation. I'm agnostic on this point. But I will note that a couple of decades ago it was widely assumed that America Online (later AOL) would be a dominant "walled garden" for internet users (at least in the USA) for the foreseeable future. Those assumptions turned out to be wrong. History suggests that multi-generational monopolies or oligopolies typically arise and last so long because they are enmeshed with the government entities that regulate them. That's not the case with regard to currently market-dominant services like Facebook or Twitter or Google (or Apple or Amazon).

most other governments around the world—feel tempted in various ways to impose content-moderation obligations on internet companies and services. (And of course they also may impose other obligations regarding the handling of personal data. [305]) Sometimes a government's demands on the technology companies may be unofficial—a warning from a Senator at a public hearing, say—but nevertheless trigger renewed efforts by tech companies to find a new balance in content moderation that will make the companies less subject to criticism. But those renewed efforts are almost invariably doomed to fail to make anyone happy, because the public response to failures in moderation is almost never to ask just to ask for less censorship of content. What's far more likely is a separate demand for different content to be censored, or for more content to be censored generally.

Nowadays some critics of the platforms want to repeal CDA 230 and sharply amend the DMCA so as to increase the risks to platforms of making bad moderation or takedown decisions. They're right that this would make the companies censor content much more—or, on the other hand, to get out of the content-moderation business (or maybe even the social-media business). But even as it's likely that more content blocking and removal by the platforms won't quell criticism, it's also possible that efforts to increase "engagement" directly with other users—as opposed to prioritizing news content itself—may lead to amplification of the very inflammatory content that (for example) Facebook's touted algorithm changes had been designed to decrease. Data from 2018 suggest that in the absence of social-media or search-engine algorithms or human editorial screeners, users themselves may use the platforms to share and promote content whose purpose is not to inform but to outrage. [306]

That a "news"-media subculture now exists whose purpose is to enflame passions rather than promote unvarnished facts is a principle insight from Benkler, Faris, and Roberts's study *Network Propaganda*, which is the subject of Chapter 19. Blaming internet media for reflecting larger media problems of the sort that *Network Propaganda* analyzes

---

305   See, e.g., the General Data Protection Regulation in the European Union or the California Consumer Privacy Act of 2018.

306   Laura Hazard Owen, *One Year In, Facebook's Big Algorithm Change Has Spurred an Angry, Fox News—Dominated—and Very Engaged!—News Feed*, Nieman Lab (Mar. 15, 2019), http://www.niemanlab.org/2019/03/one-year-in-facebooks-big-algorithm-change-has-spurred-an-angry-fox-news-dominated-and-very-engaged-news-feed/. NiemanLab is an online-reporting project of the Nieman Foundation at Harvard University.

may be appealing, but it's entirely possible that internet platforms are mirroring larger social currents that we as yet haven't recognized, much less resolved to address. So it won't be any surprise if whatever the companies do that is merely reactive to criticism will be interpreted, at best, as too little, too late.

**What the companies can do right.**   Much of my approach to the topic of regulating social media and internet companies has been focused on what we can learn from the history of societies grappling with other new mass media. If a society is already in ferment—in a period of rapid evolution and change—then a new mass medium is likely at the very least to reflect that ferment, and quite possibly to amplify it. And so it is today: the increasingly solid consensus behind the facts of global warming and climate change properly ought to lead not to debates about what has caused climatic disruption but instead to understanding what problems we can expect to result from that disruption. If climate change is a cause of increased refugee and migration floods—as it is now and will continue to be in this century—then we ought to be able to see the connection between these forced movements of populations and certain political responses in developed nations, including the rise in xenophobic anti-immigration sentiment. The internet platforms didn't cause climate change or the resultant mass population movements, but it may function sometimes as a thermometer that measures the rising political temperature. Similarly, the global financial crisis of 2008 wasn't caused by Google or Facebook or Twitter—more likely culprits include the securitization of mortgage interests buttressed by insurance against credit-default swaps, the rollback of lending regulation, and statutory incentives for lenders to grant high-risk mortgages. But populist responses to the financial crisis, which arguably include both the Occupy movement and the Tea Party movement, certainly used internet platforms to self-organize and to make their unhappiness known. The financial crisis and resultant worldwide recession arguably helped fuel the "Arab Spring" as well, and Middle East and North African (MENA) countries made a point of taking to the internet as well as to the streets to express their discontent.

But the fact that the technology companies likely weren't the proximate causes of political unrest over the last decade does not exculpate them from contributing either negligently or shortsightedly to the amplification and divisiveness of that discontent. It's an inadequate response to attacks from self-styled technology critics or media ecologists for the companies to claim that they didn't start the fires of populist rage. It's equally inadequate to respond with one-off reforms (or pledges to reform), not least because the one-off reforms won't seem to have fixed anything and in practice will make the critics more unhappy, not less.

Instead, the companies need to begin to recognize their own roles in the larger media and cultural (and physical) ecology, and to develop a systematic response aimed not at blunting criticism but at proactively engaging with it, as well as proactively contributing to solutions that address not just yesterday's and today's criticisms but also tomorrow's. In practical terms, this means beginning with my colleague Jack Balkin's insights, explored in the first four chapters of this book, about the "triangular" nature of free speech in the internet era, with speakers at one corner, government at the second corner, and internet platforms (together with other technological intermediaries) at the third corner. Understanding internet-speech problems (or internet-privacy problems) as questions of users-versus-the-government or of users-versus-the-companies is shortsighted because the governments and the companies may also be interacting with each other in less than transparent ways. As one result, government demands on technology companies may affect what the companies offer (or decline to offer) to their users in ways that are non-obvious to users. (To take one specific example, Twitter may ramp up its policing of controversial content published by users, with the result that users become unhappy with inconsistent or otherwise problematic censorship—without full awareness that Twitter's unsatisfactory interventions are a response to explicit or implicit government threats of regulation. And those threats themselves may derive from government officials' being unhappy with how they're tweeted about.)

The triangle taxonomy that Balkin outlines mandates, at the very least, that the companies must push for transparency about the extent to which their moderation policies (or privacy policies, or data-retention policies) are being driven by government demands, including informal government demands—what Balkin calls "jawboning" in his "New School Speech Regulation" paper that I discuss in Chapter 2. Many companies have already begun to publish "transparency reports," with Google (now Alphabet) having led the way. [307] But the companies can do more, and

---

307   See, *e.g., Google Transparency Report,* https://transparencyreport.google.com/.

here we look to Balkin's crucial idea of "information fiduciaries," first discussed in Chapter 4 and explored at greater length in Chapter 16.

The biggest mistake one can make with the concept of "information fiduciaries" is to imagine that any one company—even one as market-dominant as Facebook—can implement the fiduciary concept, and the strong framework of ethical commitment it entails, on its own. Imagine if Facebook adopted an "information fiduciaries" model and code of ethics that limited how the company can use our personal information as well as how it might curate what information it shows us or how it decides what information (or, perhaps more aptly, disinformation) to block, but no other companies shared that model and code of ethics. If that were to happen, the company's code of ethics would be nothing more than addendum to its Terms of Service and subject to unilateral change. It wouldn't be a framework on which anyone could rely. [308]

The better path is for the technology companies to put aside their differences and come together to develop a shared information-fiduciaries model and a shared, explicit code of ethics aimed at commitments to the duty of care (treat your users and everyone else with reasonable care and don't manipulate or exploit them), the duty of confidentiality (don't share users' personal information—or even semi-public information—without obtaining their permission, which must be revocable by the user), and the duty of loyalty (don't betray your direct relationship with users in the interest of your relationships with other parties, or out of self-interest). In the best of all possible worlds, occasional competitors and rivals would convene on their own to develop such a code of ethics as well as inter-company and inter-industry channels for policing and enforcing it. In a less-than-ideal world like the one we live in, it may take some pushes from government to motivate the companies to convene on this project. (And that's okay too.)

But keep in mind that just as it serves the tech industries to work together on issues like technical standard-setting (the kind of thing the IEEE Standards Association or the Internet Engineering Task Force does), it also would serve the companies to implement proactive fiduciary and ethics standard-setting, just as bar associations and medical association do.

---

308   It's an ethics-code version of Wittgenstein's "private language" argument, developed in *Philosophical Investigations*. The short version of this argument is that the rules you have to follow in interacting with other people have to be external to you—they have to be objective rules that are bigger than you—or else they're incoherent and unenforceable. *See Private language argument*, Wikipedia (last edited Mar. 13, 2019), https://en.wikipedia.org/wiki/Private language argument.

An Information Fiduciary Standards Association might be just the ticket. The potential benefits seem obvious: on the one hand, a commitment to a larger framework of ethical treatment of users could help restore trust in an industry where user trust recently has been shaken. And commitment to larger standards of ethics could, as I discuss primarily in Chapter 4, give the companies standing to resist, on grounds of ethical principle, the periodic government demands for either censorship or user information or both. [309]

**What the rest of us can do right.** When it comes to getting their houses in order, the tech companies have their work cut out for them. But when it comes to understanding and coping with internet media and technology companies, we as citizens have our own work to do as well. Part of that work has to teaching ourselves to have some perspective about social media, search engines, technological companies generally, and larger effects of technological change. It's an old, old joke that "everybody complains about the weather but no one does anything about it"; the equivalent line about social media might be something like "most people complain about Facebook and Twitter and Instagram but hardly anyone quits using them altogether." Even those of us who take a break from Twitter or Facebook mostly come back, which I think has to be because we find some value in these forums. Given that experience, we ought to recognize that we get a lot of benefit from the internet platforms, and to a large that benefit stems from hearing other people's voices and connecting with other people's lives. For all that some critics like Tristan Harris and Roger McNamee want to analogize the internet to chemical addictions (heroin, say, or alcohol), the hallmark of most such addictions is that people self-isolate. I want to suggest that, even if some subset of people uses social media or their digital devices addictively, for the most part those of us who spend a lot of time on the internet are reaching out to a larger world of other people, new information, and different points of view. It would be a shame, in my view, if in our reflexive impulse to condemn a new medium for problems that themselves much bigger than any medium, we hamstrung or sterilized the ability of individuals

---

309   One salutary effect of this industry commitment might be that, instead of having different tech companies snipe at each other on the question of who's better at protecting privacy—as Apple and Facebook have done in recent years—the companies could recognize that they have a common interest in protecting users' privacy and speech and autonomy and even, arguably, legal standing to defend those interests in courts or other tribunals.

to use the internet to self-organize, promote democracy, and collaborate on solutions to today's problems and tomorrow's.

The source of my vision for what's possible in terms of positive collaboration on social-media platforms and elsewhere is Wikipedia. (Full disclosure: I was general counsel for the Wikimedia Foundation for a few years and a consulting attorney for WMF for a couple of years after that.) Before Wikipedia existed, few people thought a massively collaborative encyclopedia was even possible. But Wikipedia is not only possible—it's actually quite useful, which even its loudest critics are sometimes compelled to acknowledge. What makes Wikipedia useful is that it combines (a) the free-speech protections of CDA 230 (and, to a lesser extent, the notice-and-takedown provisions of the DMCA) with (b) massive democratic participation and contribution framed by (c) a shared code of ethics, grounded in "five Pillars" [310] that can be reduced to the following:

- Wikipedia is an encyclopedia.

- Wikipedia is written from a neutral point of view.

- Wikipedia is free content that anyone can use, edit, and distribute.

- Wikipedia's editors should treat each other with respect and civility.

- Wikipedia has no firm rules.

Wikipedia, of course, is not perfect (no human enterprise is). Its five pillars aren't perfectly adhered to. Wikipedia sometimes contains false information that needs to be corrected but isn't always quickly corrected. And while it has "five pillars" and many (many!) subsidiary rules and policies, those rules are not, the "five pillars" page tells us, "carved in stone" and are meant to be able to "evolve over time."

Without CDA 230, Wikipedia couldn't exist. It also couldn't exist without a large-scale commitment to its shared principles, including ethics. It also has a built-in recognition of the need for its standards to evolve. I strongly believe the Wikipedia model suggests a path forward for internet companies that believe the positive potential of internet platforms and other technology platforms vastly outweighs the damage that can

---

310   *Wikipedia:Five pillars*, Wikipedia (last edited Mar. 7, 2019), https://en.wikipedia. org/wiki/Wikipedia:Five pillars.

be done by those who misuse them. That path involves engagement, the development and promotion of a shared ethical framework, and the recognition both of imperfection and the need to evolve. It also will require, I think, exploration of ways to engage user populations in the larger project of screening for disinformation and other garbage content, rather than simply implementing censorship non-transparently and inconsistently from the top down. The lesson of Wikipedia is that human moderation can, in fact, scale up for large internet resources if you empower users to contribute to the content-moderation progress.

This will mean hard work—we can't just close our eyes and hope our problems will evaporate or that we'll evolve past them. Yes, we absolutely must work on strategies to pro-actively fight disinformation and the deliberate dissemination of lies. (Again, see Appendix A.) But that strategy has to be informed by a faith in democracy, and faith in one another. It requires what arguably is an even more fundamental principle of Wikipedia than the "five pillars." That principle is articulated as "Wikipedia:Assume good faith." [311] I'll quote a part of that page here:

> *Assuming good faith* (AGF) is a fundamental principle on Wikipedia. It is the assumption that editors' edits and comments are made in good faith. Most people try to help the project, not hurt it. If this were untrue, a project like Wikipedia would be doomed from the beginning. This guideline does not require that editors continue to assume good faith in the presence of obvious evidence to the contrary (e.g. vandalism). Assuming good faith does not prohibit discussion and criticism. Rather, editors should not attribute the actions being criticized to malice unless there is specific evidence of such.

> When disagreement occurs, try to the best of your ability to explain and resolve the problem, not cause more conflict, and so give others the opportunity to reply in kind. Consider whether a dispute stems from different perspectives, and look for ways to reach consensus.

Despite the fashion of supposing that Facebook (or Google or Twitter or any other platform or internet service) is essentially amoral and

---

311    *Wikipedia:Assume good faith*, Wikipedia (last edited Dec. 8, 2018), https://
en.wikipedia.org/wiki/Wikipedia:Assume`good`faith.

selfish—and, to be sure, some companies have given us ample reason to think this might be true—I think it's a useful exercise to act at the outset as if we can assume they want to do good, and to act in good faith. Most of the companies' missteps I believe are grounded not in sociopathology or malice but in the arrogance that derives from their own sense that their intentions are good. That arrogance has been shaken by the "techlash," and that's all to the good—after all, we all know what the road to hell is paved with.

Ideally, the companies will respond to public criticism with engagement rather than defensiveness—and let's be realistic and anticipate that there will always be more criticism. [312] The best way for the companies to engage with its critics is for them to co-sponsor a multi-stakeholder forum specifically focused on dealing with these content and privacy issues—and invite all the critics, even the meanest ones, to participate. Lee Tomson and David Morar have argued for a "Content Congress"—a multi-stakeholder forum to surface and address everyone's concerns about internet content issues. [313] I think that's a fine idea, but I would expand it to include privacy issues as well, not least because there needs to be a counterweight to current international initiatives to regulate speech and privacy without input from all stakeholders. It could also take up the information-fiduciary proposal I discuss above and either host it or contribute to it.

My argument that Wikipedia's success can be a model for social-media reform isn't rooted in any naïve optimism about social media, the internet, or democracy. It has always been clear to me that empowering ordinary citizens to speak broadly and widely on the internet would be disruptive and troubling for many, even though I believed its larger impact would be positive. I also have long believed that democracies are inherently fragile, and we need to think through all the problems that open societies can face if we want to protect our democracies. (This is the subject of Chapter 18.) Even so, I believe that if you can take a leap of faith with me—the same kind of leap that led our culture to embrace freedom of speech and press to begin with—we can endure today's uncertainty long enough to build a better internet and technological ecology for ourselves tomorrow.

---

312   Emily Birnbaum, *Live video of New Zealand shooting puts tech on defensive*, TheHill (Mar. 16, 2019), https://thehill.com/policy/technology/434346-live-video-of-new-zealand-shooting-puts-tech-on-defensive.

313   Tomson & Morar, *supra* note 8.

That a successful, massively collaborative project like Wikipedia was even possible was hardly imagined by any of us before it happened. The internet before Wikipedia is very much like the social-media landscape today—we're so distracted by the newness of the medium and by the harm that people demonstrate they can perpetrate with it that we haven't yet envisioned how our giant communities might come together in virtual barn-raising and city-building. We need not to hobble our new tools before we've learned how best to collaborate with them. And this will mean less focus on punishing the tech companies for their failure to foresee how their systems might be abused—noting, in fairness, that most of the rest of us didn't foresee this it either—than on engaging with them and teaching them how to do better.

Of course we could always chart a different, retrogressive course—turning our backs on the potential for the internet platforms to facilitate wider-scale engagement among citizens all over the world. We could insist, as some countries are inclined to insist even now, that internet and technology companies are so dangerous that we need to hobble them (and maybe even break them up) before they become even more dangerous and out of control. We could retrofit the massively democratic internet so that your published words on Twitter or Facebook are no more likely to reach larger audiences than you are likely to get your letter to the *New York Times* printed. We could always try to turn back the clock.

But I keep coming back to the problems we face that are bigger than the internet and global in scale—like climate change, the rise of xenophobic nationalism, and the most recent global financial crisis. These problems are so big that we're going to need bigger teams of creative minds to solve them. The internet, including social media, search engines, and other shared resources—and yet increasingly available to us on devices we can carry in our pockets—still offers the greatest single tool for human beings to work together and solve large-scale problems that the world has ever seen. I've seen enough counterintuitive examples of positive internet collaboration to be certain we can use these tools better than we've done so far. What's more, I'm not sure we're going to do well in tackling global problems if we aren't free to use these digital tools to their maximum positive potential. That won't happen if we legislate incentives for the internet companies to censor more—"just to be on the safe side." And it won't happen if the companies don't publicly and aggressively commit themselves not merely to protect our privacy but to act as advocates for positive change, working with one another and with their critics to bring that change about.

I can't guarantee that I'm right about all this stuff. But I know we'll never find out if I'm right about it if we don't begin by assuming good faith.

"Well, Doctor, what have we got—a Republic or a Monarchy?" a woman asked Benjamin Franklin at the close of the Constitutional Convention of 1787. Reportedly, Franklin answered with this: "A Republic, if you can keep it."

In 1997, when I was finishing my first book, *Cyber Rights*, I had a similar view of the case, *Reno v. ACLU*, in which we'd won Supreme Court recognition of the importance of the First Amendment on the internet. If you had asked me then what we won, I'd likely have said, "free speech on the internet, if you can keep it."

Now more than ever we must work together to keep it.

# The Seven-Step Program for Fighting Disinformation

*By Renee DiResta and Mike Godwin*

This article was originally published in Just Security on Feb. 28, 2019 at https://www.justsecurity.org/62718/step-program-fighting-disinformation/

After nearly two years of investigation by Congress and the Department of Justice, there's no longer any serious dispute that Russia and other unfriendly state actors are exploiting social media, hoping to fracture Western democratic institutions and social cohesion. The question is only to what extent it's working. But whether you believe that Russian exploits shifted the outcomes in the United Kingdom's Brexit referendum or the 2016 U.S. presidential election is, oddly enough, beside the point. The hard fact is, these disruptive efforts are certain to continue, and state-level adversaries will only up their game and push harder for successful outcomes as time goes on. Neither state-actor trolls nor would-be domestic propagandists will be going away anytime soon.

That's why a comprehensive response-and-deterrence strategy is critical. One of us (DiResta) is a technical researcher, and the other (Godwin) is a civil-liberties lawyer, but we're both committed to democracy and to cybersecurity. We also share the conviction that it's time to come up with a bold, full-spectrum strategy for addressing and mitigating information operations, and that the public needs to participate in this conversation. So that's why we've decided to present our plan—Seven Steps for Fighting Disinformation—to proactively prepare for the next wave of social-media and internet-based psychological operations.

The seven steps can be summarized as follows:

1. Move past blame, and look ahead to solutions

2. Define disinformation as a cybersecurity issue, not a content problem

3. Specify protections for the rights to free expression and privacy

4. Create multi-stakeholder mechanisms for sharing threat information effectively

5. Establish a fiduciary framework to promote platform ethics and user well-being

6. Establish an oversight body (or bodies) to identify disinformation problems and strategic solutions

7. Backstop all this with civil and criminal deterrence strategies

Our First Step is simple: move past blame. Yes, the tech platforms screwed up in 2016. Yes, our media institutions got played. Our government institutions failed to recognize the full scope of the disinformation problem. But ultimately, the finger-pointing, denial, and defensiveness about past election outcomes are small-bore debates. Despite their shortfalls in 2016, the tech companies will have to be key partners in any comprehensive plan to handle disruptive social media propaganda and platform-based psychological operations. Addressing disinformation going forward requires unity and cooperation.

Our Second Step: classify disinformation as a cybersecurity problem. The problem with information operations isn't just that they are unpleasant, disagreeable, or even false—it's that their intended purpose isn't to argue or communicate, but instead to destabilize and undermine genuine argument and communication. Even provable falsehood is no good as a litmus test. The most effective propaganda frequently contains seeds of truth; the truthful elements are incorporated precisely to immunize propagandistic communications from criticism. So truth policing and fact-checking can't be this century's Maginot Line. The goal of our adversaries is corrosion, not communication – they are working to create confusion, to make it feel exhausting to determine what's true or what to trust.

No single state-actor or ideological group owns these tactics. Russia's operation is the most widely analyzed and publicly discussed, but it's only one example of a wide-ranging collection of documented information attacks, scaled from the very large to the very small. What distinguishes today's disinformation operations isn't where they comes from, but how they're executed: the systematic manipulation and exploitation of social network dissemination capabilities, often leveraging tactics used by spammers and malware creators. The tactics evolve rapidly, and new vulnerabilities emerge as platform features and technology change. That's why we have to treat disinformation as a cybersecurity problem, learning to detect dissemination signatures characteristic of deliberate deceptions, distortions, and other intentionally disruptive measures. A cybersecurity mindset doesn't just enable us to spot problems—it also helps us craft solutions. This includes establishing ethical, industry-accepted framework for "red-team" methodologies to identify vulnerabilities, which will enable us to be proactive rather than endlessly reactive.

Our Third Step: Any U.S. anti-disinformation strategy has to be designed with preserving both freedom of expression and privacy as a top priority. Disinformation isn't merely "speech we disapprove of." We can't let genuine differences of political opinion (or other kinds of opinion) become collateral damage as we detect and root out disinformation campaigns. At the same time, we also have to remember that bad actors will insist, disingenuously, that what we do to combat disinformation is censorship. To defang these narratives, addressing disinformation campaigns must be done as transparently as possible. Platform companies must inform the public about what we're all doing to combat disinformation. Frameworks similar to the practice of making Digital Millennium Copyright Act [314] takedowns publicly accessible (both individually and collectively) provide a good starting point. This would allow the platforms to demonstrate that any takedown is done with care toward protecting the right of the people to speak freely, to preserve privacy, and to associate with one another on the internet as well as elsewhere.

---

314   Digital Millennium Copyright Act, 17 U.S.C. § 512.

The first three Steps establish a common understanding of the threat. The Fourth Step moves us toward building tangible infrastructure for addressing the problem. We must establish multi-stakeholder bodies to construct standards and promote clearly defined accountabilities and oversight. We already have good examples of dedicated, formalized multi-stakeholder structures for cooperation and threat information sharing between the public and private sectors–successful models like the Cyber Threat Alliance (CTA); and the National Telecommunications and Information Administration's (NTIA) Multi-stakeholder Collaboration on Vulnerability Research Disclosure. We should build on these models, enabling government agencies and tech companies to share their evolving knowledge of disinformation tactics and defense strategies with one another.

The evolving nature of information attacks leads to our Fifth Step: platforms must agree to prioritize ethics and user wellbeing. Godwin has argued that the social-media companies should answer rising concern about disinformation and privacy breaches by adopting a standard, shared professional code of ethics in the same way that doctors, lawyers, and other professions are bound by law and ethics[315] to do. Obviously, legislators and regulators can and should impose duties on the companies to be proactive in protecting consumer well-being and preventing the rampant spread of disinformation. The companies might reactively oppose these duties, but we argue they should instead embrace them. The more voluntary the companies adoption of "information fiduciary" duties is, the better—not only do we need the companies' input to strike the right balance (and protect free expression and privacy), but enthusiastic embrace of a fiduciary role could also restore the public trust in the companies that prior lapses have eroded.

The Sixth Step is oversight—a necessary measure to ensure that platforms remain accountable. By ensuring third-party oversight with teeth, we can verify that tech companies are doing their utmost to manage and mitigate pervasive disinformation and manipulation in our privately owned public squares. The integrity of their products is increasingly tied to the information integrity that undergirds our democracy. Because bad actors will develop new tactics and strategies as internet platforms continue to evolve, we must ensure that the tech

---

315   Godwin, *supra* note 12.

companies are incentivized to remain proactive in assuming responsibility for addressing disinformation on their platforms.

To establish this oversight, Congress needs to come together in bipartisan consensus and take action. That may be a challenge—recent Congressional investigative hearings have exposed knowledge gaps and devolved into partisan bickering. But, reaching further back into its rich history, Congress also has shown its potential to overcome partisan division and pass targeted solutions. Among current proposals, we endorse the Honest Ads Act [316] from Senators Warner and Klobuchar as a good first step toward regulating political advertising online to reduce the risk of manipulation. Senator Warner's 20 Policy Proposals [317] point the way to more measures with potential to clean up social media disinformation, protect user data, improve media literacy education, and make bots more visible.

But Congress can't be expected to do all this alone. To restore integrity to our information ecosystem, we need strategic defense planning and deterrence frameworks in addition to private-public collaboration and platform accountability.

That brings us to our Seventh Step—the need for a criminal-law and civil-liability framework to establish deterrence. There are currently no direct and consistent consequences for running influence operations, and therefore no downside to attempting them. The sheer variety, scope, and range of actors makes the argument for a whole-of-government cybersecurity doctrine, with deployed tools to detect and respond to malign influence campaigns. We need to better align government resources to address what are currently asymmetric threats. At a minimum, the President should start by immediately reinstating a cybersecurity coordinator on the National Security Council.

We're not claiming to have gotten everything right with our Seven Step Program for overcoming disinformation, but we hope to spark a conversation about how our new democratic media are being used to corrode democratic societies. Just as the widespread adoption of the automobile forced society to think harder about how to cope with accidents, traffic jams, and safety regulations, we need to plan deliberately,

---

316   Honest Ads Act, S. 1989, 115th Cong. (Oct. 19, 2017).

317   Ariel Shapiro, *Democratic Sen. Warner Has a New Policy Paper with Proposals to Regulate Big Tech Companies*, CNBC (July 30, 2018), https://www.cnbc.com/2018/07/30/sen-warner-proposes-20-ways-to-regulate-big-tech-and-radically-change.html.

in an ongoing way, for how we will contain this downside to our new social communication infrastructure. And just as the United States and other countries have had to deal with domestic as well as foreign terrorists, we face domestic as well as foreign disinformation campaigns. This means we need to put aside partisan divisions and commit to a shared program of anticipating, responding to, and deterring the threat of deliberate manipulation campaigns.

We believe that we can build an effective response to disinformation without eroding or undermining fundamental values such as freedom of expression online. But first we must resolve—as experts, company leaders, legislators, judges, regulators, and individual citizens—to build it.

# Godwin's Law: Then and Now

Periodically I'm asked to write about one of my inventions that seems to have a life of its own with regard to social media and democracy. That invention is Godwin's Law, a "memetic engineering" experiment I worked up in the early days of online communications, predating the public internet. The purpose of Godwin's Law was (and still is) to discourage people engaged in online discussions from trivializing Nazis, Hitler, or the Holocaust with gratuitous inappropriate comparisons.

What Godwin's Law emphatically *isn't*—despite how it is sometimes interpreted in social media and elsewhere on the internet (and in popular culture generally)—is a prohibition of any comparisons invoking Hitler, Nazis, or the Holocaust. Sometimes such comparisons make sense. And if we shouldn't trivialize history because it provides important lessons for the present, we shouldn't fear or forget history either. And we shouldn't avoid historical comparisons when appropriate, as they may have something useful to teach us. These two essays, one from late 2015 and one from mid-2018, may be taken as bookends to certain abrupt shifts towards populism, nationalism, and even isolationism that emerged in 2016's elections, both in the United States and elsewhere in the world. Social media and democracy certainly can bear, and should tolerate, thoughtful invocations of history, including, when appropriate recognition of the parallels between modern-day belligerent nationalism and its historical precursors from the middle of the last century.

In short, I include these short essays to anticipate questions from some readers as to whether I've revised my thinking about Godwin's Law in the fact of current developments in public discourse on the internet and in democratic culture generally. I don't think I have, but I'll let you be the judge.

# Sure, call Trump a Nazi. Just make sure you know what you're talking about.

This article was originally published in *The Washington Post* on December 14, 2015, at https://www.washingtonpost.com/posteverything/wp/2015/12/14/sure-call-trump-a-nazi-just-make-sure-you-know-what-youre-talking-about/

First, let me get this Donald Trump issue out of the way: If you're thoughtful about it and show some real awareness of history, go ahead and refer to Hitler or Nazis when you talk about Trump. Or any other politician.

My Facebook timeline and Twitter feed have been blowing up lately. And whenever that happens, it's almost always because someone's making comparisons to Hitler or Nazis or the Holocaust somewhere. Sure enough, as Trump pontificates about immigrants or ethnic or religious minorities, with scarcely less subtlety than certain early 20th-century political aspirants in Europe did, people on the Internet feel compelled to ask me what I think about it.

Why? Simple: Because 25 years ago, when the Internet was still a pup, I came up with Godwin's Law. In its original form, Godwin's Law goes like this: "As an online discussion continues, the probability of a reference or comparison to Hitler or Nazis approaches 1."

Invoking Hitler or Nazis (or World War II or the Holocaust) is common in public life these days, both in the United States and around the world, and it has been for quite a while. Back in 1990, I set out — half-seriously and half-whimsically — to do something about it.

Through most of the 1980s, I'd been a hobbyist using computer "bulletin-board systems" that connected small local communities by telephone lines. I couldn't help but notice how often comparisons to Hitler or Nazis came up in heated exchanges, usually as a kind of rhetorical hammer to express rage or contempt for one's opponent. Once I was back in school to study law, I leveraged my student status to get a free Internet-based computer account. With access to the global Internet came still more hyperbolic Hitler and Nazi comparisons.

Despite the Internet's distractions, I did actually manage to study law. And I was drawn to a particular kind of legal problem: What happens when a nation, although acting consistently with its own laws, behaves so monstrously that other nations, and eventually history itself, are compelled to condemn it? I steeped myself in the history of the Nazi movement and in accounts of the Holocaust, including Primo Levi's harrowing *Survival in Auschwitz.* I was increasingly troubled by the disconnect between what I was reading about the Third Reich and the way people used that era against debating opponents online.

Could I help close the gap between the glibness and the graphic accounts? I was no historian or eyewitness; I probably knew less about Hitler and Nazi Germany than the average viewer of the History Channel. But I knew enough about science to recast my distaste for these trivializing comparisons as if it were a law of nature. I framed Godwin's Law as a pseudo-mathematical probability statement, almost like a law of physics. I wanted to hint that most people who brought Nazis into a debate about, say, New York Gov. Andrew Cuomo's views on gun control weren't being thoughtful and independent. Instead, they were acting just as predictably, and unconsciously, as a log rolling down a hill.

After some early energetic seeding on my part, "Godwin's Law" took off in the early days of large-scale public access to the Internet. Users would see a poorly reasoned, hyperbolic invocation of Nazis or the Holocaust and call the arguer to account, claiming the shallow argument had proved (or, sometimes, had "violated") Godwin's Law. Soon after, Godwin's Law propagated into the mainstream media as well. Democrats and Republicans alike invoke it from time to time — so do other political parties in the United States and around the world. Sometimes it's invoked by a Democratic blogger; sometimes it's cited by a Republican. The law notably surfaced recently in Canadian politics, too.

So has Godwin's Law actually reduced spurious Hitler or Nazi or Holocaust comparisons? Obviously not — just sample your own media sources, and you'll find that Hitler comparisons are alive and well. (My personal favorite this year: the Mets fan who likened Yankees fans to former Nazi Party members.) But I do think the meme gives Internet users a clear opportunity to think critically about shallow references to the Nazis or the Holocaust. And it exposes glib Nazi comparisons or Holocaust references to the harsh light of interrogation.

The idea seems to travel well, adapting itself to new languages and cultures. In French, for example, users sometimes say a debate has reached "the Godwin point" when discussion has degenerated into Nazi comparisons, and one author, François De Smet, subtitled his 2014 book *Reductio ad Hitlerum* (a philosophical essay) as "une théorie du point Godwin."

To be clear: I don't personally believe all rational discourse has ended when Nazis or the Holocaust are invoked. But I'm pleased that people still use Godwin's Law to force one another to argue more thoughtfully. The best way to prevent future holocausts, I believe, is not to forbear from Holocaust comparisons; instead, it's to make sure that those comparisons are meaningful and substantive. This is something a pleasantly surprising percentage of commentators in this political season have managed to do (like this piece on Trump by New America and CNN analyst Peter Bergen). [318] And I'm pleased in any season to see more people revisiting the history books.

It's still true, of course, that the worst thing you can say about your opponents, in our culture, is that they're like Hitler or the Nazis. But I'm hopeful that we can prod our glib online rhetorical culture into a more thoughtful, historically reflective space. In 2015, the Internet gives more and more individuals both the information and the skepticism to question what politicians and others say in their Hitler-centered hyperboles. Just as importantly, the Internet gives us the tools to share

---

318    Bergen, P. (2019). *Is Donald Trump a fascist?* CNN. Available at: https://www.cnn.com/2015/12/09/opinions/bergen-is-trump-fascist/index.html [Accessed 30 Apr. 2019].

our criticisms — including the appropriately appalled reaction to Trump's statements — with one another more widely.

The one thing we shouldn't be skeptical of is our right — our obligation, even — as ordinary individuals to use the Internet and the other tools of the digital age to challenge our would-be leaders and check the facts.

And by all means be skeptical of Godwin's Law, too. But you don't need me to tell you that.

# Do we need to update Godwin's Law about the probability of comparison to Nazis?

This article was originally published in *The Los Angeles Times* on June 24, 2018, at https://www.latimes.com/opinion/op-ed/la-oe-godwin-godwins-law-20180624-story.html

D oes Godwin's Law need to be updated? Suspended? Repealed? I get asked this question from time to time because I'm the guy who came up with it more than a quarter century ago.

In its original simple form, Godwin's Law goes like this: "As an online discussion continues, the probability of a comparison to Hitler or to Nazis approaches one." It's deliberately pseudo-scientific — meant to evoke the Second Law of Thermodynamics and the inevitable decay of physical systems over time. My goal was to hint that those who escalate a debate into Adolf Hitler or Nazi comparisons may be thinking lazily, not adding clarity or wisdom, and contributing to the decay of an argument over time.

Godwin's Law doesn't belong to me, and nobody elected me to be in charge of it. Although I'm sometimes thought to be referee for its use, I'm not. That said, I do have thoughts about how it is being invoked nowadays.

Since it was released into the wilds of the internet in 1991, Godwin's Law (which I nowadays abbreviate to "GL") has been frequently reduced to a blurrier notion: that whenever someone compares anything current to Nazis or Hitler it means the discussion is over, or that that person lost the argument. It's also sometimes used (reflexively, lazily) to suggest that anyone who invokes a comparison to Nazis or Hitler has somehow "broken" the Law, and thus demonstrated their failure to grasp what made the Holocaust uniquely horrific.

Most recently GL has been invoked in response to the Trump administration's "zero tolerance" border policy that resulted in the traumatic separation of would-be immigrants from their children, many of whom are now warehoused in tent cities or the occasional repurposed Walmart. For example, former CIA and NSA director Michael Hayden — no squishy bleeding heart — posted a couple of tweets on June 16 that likened that policy to the Nazis' treatment of children in Germany's concentration camps. California Sen. Dianne Feinstein (a Democrat but also a security hawk) has made the comparison as well.

The response has been predictable: Debate for some people has been derailed by the trivial objection that, even if it is terrible to separate children from their parents (and sometimes lose track of them, or make it impossible for their parents contact them, or even deprive them of the comfort of human touch), it's not as awful as what the Nazis did. Or as bad as the slave trade. Or as bad as what the expansion of the United States westward did to Native Americans.

My name gets cited in a lot of these discussions. And of course my ears are burning. It hasn't mattered that I've explained GL countless times. Some critics on the left have blamed me for (supposedly) having shut down valid comparisons to the Holocaust or previous atrocities. Some on the right have insisted that I'm "PC" for having tweeted (a bit profanely) that it's just fine to compare the white nationalists who plagued Charlottesville, Va., last year to Nazis. (I think they were mostly aspirational Nazi cosplayers.)

I don't take either strain of criticism too seriously. But I do want to stress that the question of evil, understood historically, is bigger than party politics. GL is about remembering history well enough to draw parallels — sometimes with Hitler or with Nazis, sure — that are deeply considered. That matter. Sometimes those comparisons are going to be appropriate, and on those occasions GL should function less as a conversation ender and more as a conversation starter.

So let me start another conversation here. Take the argument that our treatment of those seeking asylum at our border, including children, is not as monstrous as institutionalized genocide. That may be true, but it's not what you'd call a compelling defense. Similarly, saying (disingenuously) that the administration is just doing what immigration law demands sounds suspiciously like "we were just following orders." That argument isn't a good look on anyone.

The seeds of future horrors are sometimes visible in the first steps a government takes toward institutionalizing cruelty. In his 1957 book *Language of the Third Reich*, Victor Klemperer recounted how, at the beginning of the Nazi regime, he "was still so used to living in a state governed by the rule of law" that he couldn't imagine the horrors yet to come. "Regardless of how much worse it was going to get," he added, "everything which was later to emerge in terms of National Socialist attitudes, actions and language was already apparent in embryonic form in these first months."

So I don't think GL needs to be updated or amended. It still serves us as a tool to recognize specious comparisons to Nazism — but also, by contrast, to recognize comparisons that aren't. And sometimes the comparisons can spot the earliest symptoms of horrific "attitudes, actions and language" well before our society falls prey to the full-blown disease.

By all means cite GL if you think some Nazi comparison is baseless, needlessly inflammatory or hyperbolic. But Godwin's Law was never meant to block us from challenging the institutionalization of cruelty or the callousness of officials who claim to be just following the law. It definitely wasn't meant to shield our leaders from being slammed for the current fashion of pitching falsehoods as fact. These behaviors, distressing as they are, may not yet add up to a new Reich, but please forgive me for worrying that they're the "embryonic form" of a horror we hoped we had put behind us.

# Selected Index